479-9613
(2)

W9-CMR-282

MARY RILEY STYLES PUBLIC LIBRARY
120 NORTH VIRGINIA AVENUE
FALLS CHURCH, VA 22046
(703) 248-5030

# REAL IRISH FOOD

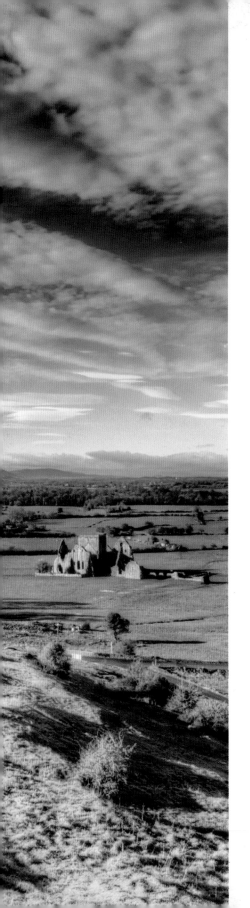

# REAL IRISH FOOD

## 150

*Classic Recipes from*
*the Old Country*

## DAVID BOWERS

Skyhorse Publishing

For Hugh and Pearse

Copyright © 2012 by David Bowers

All Rights Reserved. No part of this book may be reproduced in any manner without the express written consent of the publisher, except in the case of brief excerpts in critical reviews or articles. All inquiries should be addressed to Skyhorse Publishing, 307 West 36th Street, 11th Floor, New York, NY 10018.

Skyhorse Publishing books may be purchased in bulk at special discounts for sales promotion, corporate gifts, fund-raising, or educational purposes. Special editions can also be created to specifications. For details, contact the Special Sales Department, Skyhorse Publishing, 307 West 36th Street, 11th Floor, New York, NY 10018 or info@skyhorsepublishing.com.

Skyhorse® and Skyhorse Publishing® are registered trademarks of Skyhorse Publishing, Inc.®, a Delaware corporation.

Visit our website at www.skyhorsepublishing.com.

10 9 8 7 6 5 4 3 2 1

Library of Congress Cataloging-in-Publication Data is available on file.
ISBN: 978-1-61608-870-5

Printed in China

# METRIC AND IMPERIAL CONVERSIONS

| Ingredient | Cups/Tablespoons/Teaspoons | Ounces | Grams/Milliliters |
|---|---|---|---|
| Baking Soda | 1 cup | 8 ounces | 221 grams |
| Butter | 1 cup = 16 tablespoons = 2 sticks | 8 ounces | 230 grams |
| Cornstarch | 1 tablespoon | 0.3 ounce | 8 grams |
| Flour, all-purpose | 1 cup/1 tablespoon | 4.5 ounces/0.3 ounce | 125 grams/8 grams |
| Fruit, dried | 1 cup | 4 ounces | 120 grams |
| Liquids: cream, milk, water, or juice | 1 cup | 8 fluid ounces | 240 ml |
| Oats | 1 cup | 5.5 ounces | 150 grams |
| Spices: cinnamon, cloves, ginger, or nutmeg (ground) | 1 teaspoon | 0.2 ounce | 5 ml |
| Sugar, white | 1 cup/1 tablespoon | 7 ounces/0.5 ounce | 200 grams/12.5 grams |
| Vanilla extract | 1 teaspoon | 0.2 ounce | 4 grams |

## OVEN TEMPERATURES

| Fahrenheit | Celcius | Gas Mark |
|---|---|---|
| 225° | 110° | ¼ |
| 250° | 120° | ½ |
| 275° | 140° | 1 |
| 300° | 150° | 2 |
| 325° | 160° | 3 |
| 350° | 180° | 4 |
| 375° | 190° | 5 |
| 400° | 200° | 6 |
| 425° | 220° | 7 |
| 450° | 230° | 8 |

# CONTENTS

# INTRODUCTION

Ireland is a stunningly beautiful country. First-time visitors are always surprised to see the grass really is emerald green, and that it stays that way through the year. In the spring, bluebells sprout so profusely the gardens are a dense blue haze. Summer is a riot of foliage and morning birdsong. Autumn is full of soft mists and glowing light, and winter brings on picturesque hoarfrost that covers the hedges like icing. Everywhere you look, there's an MGM movie set of land and water and sky.

But when I think of Ireland, I think of food.

Brown soda bread so moist it barely needs the yolk-yellow butter; sweet, briny oysters so fresh they quiver on the shells; fragrant apple tarts under tender, golden crusts; rich, heartwarming stews redolent of meaty gravy and nut-sweet carrots; crisp-edged potato cakes flipped hot from a cast-iron skillet directly onto your plate.

Forget meatloaf and macaroni and cheese—this stuff is the original comfort food.

Real Irish food is more in the style of traditional French country food—not the formalized cooking of chefs, but the classic dishes with regional variations passed down from generations of home cooks. Each bonne femme's variation on boeuf en daube finds its counterpart in Irish stew, the countless versions of tartes au citron and mousses au chocolat are echoed by very distinct apple tarts and fruitcakes, and that extra fillip that gives life to a regional saucisson can be seen in each artisanal black pudding. Real Irish food is full of flavor and subtlety, based on prime ingredients treated with care and respect. Real Irish food is astonishing in its depth and range and mastery.

In the same way Italian food is about more than spaghetti and meatballs, real Irish food is a far more complex and exciting thing than the corned-beef-and-cabbage caricature we tend to think of in North America.

I know because I grew up eating the glories of Irish food, and I've missed it nearly every day of the last 20 years I have lived in the United States.

Based on my experience of St. Patrick's Day dinners in the US, I can forgive any American for expecting real Irish cooking to be boring and bland. All that watery cabbage? Ugh, no thanks.

Happily, those once-a-year cooks are wrong about nearly everything (and one of them, whom I had to re-educate, was my own American wife!). Over the last 20 years, we have continued to divide our time between Ireland and the US, spending a good deal of time in Ireland, both living there and traveling around, and always eating, eating, eating. Indeed, one of the great pleasures of our culinary life was watching the face of our oldest son when, as a toddler, he gnawed on his first Irish sausage with a look of wonder while he joyfully repeated the Irish Gaelic word for sausage I'd just taught him: "Ispini! Ispini! Ispini!"

My parents have been the source of endless education about real Irish food from both coasts. My mother is from County Mayo, on the west coast of Ireland, one of the few places where the Irish language is still spoken and almost a land unto itself in its regional isolation. My father, in his day, was a home cook so proficient I can only describe him as smokin'. He was born and bred in Dublin, the heart of the country (from anywhere else in Ireland, one goes "up to Dublin"—to all other places, one goes "down the country"). Together, my parents raised a family of four sons who are serious eaters and cooks—half of us professionals.

Between my mom and dad alone, I sampled an enormous range of dishes and regional styles at a young age. From them, I also learned surprising culinary trivia, such as the fact that black pepper was unknown in the Ireland of their youth. White pepper was the usual seasoning, and black pepper didn't appear regularly in stores and markets until the 1960's, when it was considered a daring and Italianate seasoning.

From them and my grandparents, I learned about the bastible, the cast-iron pot that served as a stove in traditional Irish cottages, and the moist and flavorful soda bread that emerges from it after half an hour over a turf fire. Growing up in Ireland, I learned to appreciate the beauty of Irish fruits and berries, which grow beautifully in a cold, damp climate—from wild strawberries and blueberries dotting the hillsides to the first crop of enormous golden raspberries, bursting with flavor, and cooking apples that practically beg to be made into cakes and tarts. And I have a terrific North Dublin recipe for Irish stew that includes fluffy, raisin-flecked dumplings. I learned about seafood, that at home we call "leppin' fresh," from the pale pink tones of true wild salmon (the dark red color of farmed salmon comes from their feed) to enormous scallops with the roe still attached. Even today, every trip back home to an Irish kitchen leaves me amazed at the incredible variety of foods, the caliber of ingredients, and the ingenuity of Irish cooks.

Most Irish people are horrified by what Americans think of as "Irish food." That's because the real thing is much subtler, more infinite in variety, and more tantalizing and seductive than any parsley-sprinkled platter of overcooked meat and mushy vegetables could ever hope to be. A prominent Irish chef told me recently, "When I was studying at Johnson and Wales in America, my roommate's family invited me for dinner, and they said, 'We're making your favorite meal!' It was corned beef and cabbage, and I had literally never heard of it before."

Real Irish food is influenced by traditions dating back to the Middle Ages, when monks made the rigors of silence and celibacy more palatable with moist, honey-sweetened oatcakes and fortified themselves against pillaging invaders by brewing up heartwarming soups, dense with barley and vegetables. And centuries before that, the Brehon laws enshrined the cow as the most valuable piece of property a Hibernian could own, marking butter and milk and certainly beef as foodstuffs to be treasured and celebrated. (It's a sentiment anyone would endorse today when tasting Ireland's bright-yellow, low-moisture butter, the result of grass-fed cows. What's more, in Ireland this isn't a premium product—it's just butter.)

In the eighteenth and nineteenth centuries, landowners and "strong farmers" ate a diet that would be sophisticated even today, from elaborate meat and vegetable preparations to a glittering array of desserts, sweets, and imported wines. There were almonds and lemons and oranges, even artichokes, as well as fresh herb omelets (called "amblets" in some old cookbook manuscripts), rich cakes full of butter and sugar, rice and pasta, often called simply "paste" but also known as macaroni, no matter what shape, dressed with plenty of butter, cream, and "toasted cheese."

Until recent years, Irish cooking always meant home cooking. There wasn't a restaurant scene because Ireland was not only a poor country for most of the last century, but also a country with a strong socialist streak, and for a long time, restaurants were considered extravagant.  In the last decade, Ireland's restaurants have undergone an astonishing culinary renaissance. More and more chefs have returned from far-flung work and travel, bringing home novel ideas for transforming Irish ingredients while mining the depths of their own native cuisine to produce food that is both home-cooked and surprisingly sophisticated.

Firm and succulent Dublin Bay prawns and sweet-fleshed west-coast lobsters once took the first plane to Paris for top prices. Now they stay at home on the tables of appreciative gourmets. A country-wide movement toward organic produce, local meats, and artisan-produced items such as cheeses, breads, and chocolate—spurred in part by a concern about genetically modified food—has led to ever wider availability and quality of staples. What about potatoes? They're everywhere, it's true, but they're prepared in countless different manners unknown to Americans.

Like the spectacle-wearing, shy girl in some 1950's movie, Irish food has flung off the dowdy trappings and emerged an elegant beauty. Ireland is now a place of destination restaurants and cooking schools, a place where foreign cooks find inspiration. From hearty stews of slow-cooked meats to innovative vegetable dishes, from trays of fresh-baked, buttery scones to dense, eggy cakes and jams bursting with tart fruit, I can think of no food so warm and welcoming, so homey and family-oriented, so truly mouth-wateringly satisfying as real Irish food.

## Irish Food in America

So where did Americans get the idea Irish food is dull? Consider that many, many Irish-Americans trace their heritage back to the poverty-stricken people who fled Ireland during a horrific famine in the 1840's. It's no wonder the dishes that survived in America were rough-and-ready peasant food, created to offer as much bulk and sustenance as possible at the least expense. It's the same with pasta, which Italian-Americans serve as an entire, filling meal, but which in Italy, is treated as a delicate, lightly sauced first course.

As in any culture, however, subsistence food is only part of the culinary story and has regrettably left Irish food not exactly shining. It has consistently been unsung, underappreciated, and dismissed. Irish stew, which much-missed British chef Keith Floyd once wrote would be heralded around the world had the French invented it, is mocked, unmanned, and dishonored by the watery, unmeaty versions of it purveyed in the name of Ireland by people who have never set foot on the island.

In fact, I would go so far as to place the blame squarely on corned beef for the less-than-stellar reputation that Irish food has in America. Every March 17, millions of people eat soggy cabbage and salty beef in the mistaken belief they're paying some sort of painful culinary homage to Ireland. They'd be closer to the mark (and doubtless happier) with a pint of Guinness, a dozen fresh oysters, a sliced lemon, and some buttered brown bread. And Ireland hasn't helped matters. They have allowed certain food myths to take hold by feeding busloads of tourists the worst sort of steam-tray potatoes and overcooked roast beef and breakfasted them on bland, lumpy porridge, brown bread, and "the truly criminal," as Irish novelist Mary Lavin wrote, "cheap jam."

I believe there are some souls in the west of Ireland, around County Clare, who actually do corn beef and eat it with cabbage. At best, it's a highly specific regional dish. What the Irish do eat more generally across the country is bacon and cabbage, which looks sort of like corned beef but is so much tastier. It's made from the "collar," which is, to American pork butchers, the butt end of the picnic. The collar is lightly cured, then simmered with vegetables until tender and delicate, and served with what the Irish call "spring cabbage," the very dark green first shoots of what will later be large cabbage heads. Because spring cabbage is tender, lightly cooked as it should be, and dressed with a little butter, it is miles away from a tough head of white cabbage boiled into submission.

So how can Americans possibly reproduce bacon and cabbage, or any other Irish dish that's based on local ingredients, in their own kitchens? It can be done, with a little ingenuity and care. For instance, lightly brined Boston butt tastes almost identical to Irish bacon, and a mixture of very lightly sautéed and steamed curly kale or savoy cabbage offers a much more Irish flavor.

Fortunately, reproducing most classic Irish food doesn't involve much sleight of hand, but it's good to know it can be done when necessary. And the extra effort is well worth it. Tasting Irish food the way it's meant to be tasted is nothing less than an eye-opening experience.

In this book, you'll find a sweeping review of Irish cuisine, from food the Irish have been eating for centuries—such as porridge with cream, heart-warming beef stews, and cakes laden with dried fruit and warm spices, as well as delectable sweets made with almonds and oranges—to foods we've eaten merely for decades, such as holiday roast turkey with a distinctive sausage stuffing and the classic Irish breakfast of rashers, sausages, and fried eggs with grilled tomatoes and mushrooms (the black and white puddings, also integral, date back to much longer ago). Other dishes are even more recent but still hallowed in the Irish kitchen—Irish coffee, for example, was dreamed up by a bartender at Shannon Airport but is now served in any pub, consumed with great gusto by tourists and locals alike, and often caps the end of an Irish dinner party.

No matter how old or new, what's here is real Irish food, the real stuff that people all across Ireland eat all the time (or at every holiday). And real Irish country food, like the real country foods of France and Italy, is about careful and frugal preparations to bring out the best of locally available ingredients, with time-honored and traditional recipes.

I've designed the recipes in this book so you can get good results in an American kitchen and an authentic feel of classic Irish dishes, even without Irish ingredients. Many tourists come home excited about the wonderful meals they've eaten in Ireland. They want to reproduce the wonderfully moist and nutty brown soda bread the landlady in their B&B whipped up for breakfast every morning before her eyes were even open, or they're looking for butter that's as flavorful and golden as what they got in their travels. But by following the recipe exactly in their American kitchens, even measuring out the whole-wheat flour by weight instead of measuring by cup, they merely get a pale brown bread, not particularly nutty or moist, topped with butter that seems white and flavorless by comparison, and they're sadly disappointed. With the recipes here, you can reproduce the flavor, the texture, and, more importantly, the nutty moistness of typical Irish brown bread, and even, with surprisingly little difficulty, churn your own cultured butter!

Same with Irish stew. If the version served in American pubs on St. Patrick's Day hasn't impressed you much, try the real thing, made with lamb chops layered with thinly sliced potatoes and onions (no carrots), seasoned well, and slow-cooked in a covered pot with very little liquid. The delicate flavor, the perfectly cooked vegetables, and the tender meat will show better than any description why the Irish get so excited about stew.

You'll find all the classics here, from barmbrack and brown scones to the old-fashioned Dublin favorite, gur cake, a sweet, sticky filling of cake crumbs, fruit, and syrup encased in tender pastry, beloved of generations of schoolchildren. There are recipes for every type of soda bread around the country, from the austere cakes of flour, buttermilk, soda and salt, to the egg, butter, and fruit-enriched versions designed for flush times, and the caraway-seeded cakes from the south, not to mention the "yellow-meal" (cornmeal) soda breads that date back to famine times when cornmeal was imported in an attempt to feed the starving.

You'll also find recipes for everything the Irish do to a potato, from the simplest boiling (still peeled at the table, dipped in salt, and occasionally even dipped in buttermilk, the real peasant tradition) to the most elaborate champs, colcannon, poundies, boxty, and cakes, as well as a favorite fall dish, Potato-Apple Cake, a sort of dense tart. If you're wondering what that "cally" was your Irish granny used to talk about, here's the book to find out how to make it yourself (potatoes mashed with butter, cream, and the first of the tender summer scallions, of course). Can't find anything to reproduce the flavor of those juicy and mild-flavored little sausages that appear on every Irish breakfast table? Make your own in the food processor or with the meat-grinder attachment on your fancy mixer. (You'll also learn how to make traditional Irish black and white pudding, should you be so inclined, or simply where to buy either in the United States in Sources, p. 21.)

Throw away your Boston grandmother's recipe for mushy veggies and discover a method of cooking that's fresh and simple, homey and comforting, from warm, soothing honest breads and cakes, to original and inviting vegetables, with grace notes of exquisite seafood and delectable roast meats. You will also discover fascinating bits of Irish culinary history, from country remedies for coughs and colds to festive dishes and special feasts. The old saying goes that everyone is a little bit Irish on St. Patrick's Day, and with any recipe here, you'll be glad to claim that heritage.

## What Makes Irish Food Special?

Cool, wet climates aren't usually considered good for growing. In Ireland, however, the weather creates unparalleled strawberries, red and golden raspberries, tangy blackberries free for the taking along every country roadside, and fragrant wild blueberries, known as fraughans (FROCK-ens).

Not to mention there are apples galore, from the delicately perfumed Cox's orange pippins, typically served with nothing more than a fruit knife, to the lumpy, misshapen Bramleys, a cooking apple whose tart, meaty flesh, the true essence of apple, makes a Golden Delicious taste like papery mush.

Classic Irish food showcases this harvest of cool weather better than any other culture: carrots, onions, parsnips, and other root vegetables of an unsurpassed sweetness, all types of potatoes bursting their skins with floury, flavorful goodness, fruits I dare any other country to match, and meat that still tastes of meat. Irish dairy products include a rich and bright yellow butter with the highest fat content, more flavorful than anything to be found in Normandy. Like the French, the Irish culture the cream slightly before churning, and the resulting golden block of butter is a condiment, a spread, and a sauce in its own right. Irish eggs have the dark orange yolk of the real organic, free-range egg, and Irish beef is truly grass-fed, with the chewy, beefy flavor so lacking in corn-fed meat.

The best American chefs insist on knowing the source of their ingredients, and they spend time and effort hunting out local suppliers, but the average Irish village inhabitant can walk into the local butcher shop and buy a piece of beef, pork, or lamb that likely came from the butcher's own flock or that of one of his family members.

Fishmongers at any town near the coast (and since it's a pretty small island, many towns are near the coast) can supply seafood and shellfish straight off a boat that same day, and sometimes they smoke their own salmon into the bargain. Eggs and dairy products are antibiotic and hormone-free, and usually organic, even at the largest supermarkets.

It is, truly, a gourmet's paradise.

But what do home cooks do back in the kitchen with all this fresh, seasonal, organic bounty? They transform it into a huge and fascinating range of foods. Give any type of artist absolute freedom, an unlimited budget and endless approval, and most of them will end up paralyzed with indecision.

But impose strict limitations—and creativity flows. (Look at Michelangelo: He never did better work than when some patron was breathing down his neck, or his block of marble was flawed.) Thus the traditional Irish cook found endless and infinitely delicious variety within basic vegetables and fruits, a simple range of meats and poultry, an abbreviated list of herbs and spices, good eggs and dairy, and excellent grains.

## Regional Differences and Classic Dishes

From these building blocks of the classic Irish kitchen, what riches have flowed! Ireland is a small place (about the size of Maine). It doesn't have the range in produce of a country the size of France, where you'll find goose fat and winey richness in Quercy and the Périgord; zesty, herb-and-olive-oil Mediterranean flavors in Provence; and butterfat, apple cider, and tender tarts in Normandy. Instead, Ireland's regions came up with dramatically different regional styles for similar ingredients, from the boxty (a sort of crepe) of Ulster in the north, to the caraway-studded buttery potato cakes of Munster in the South, to the meaty stews of Leinster, and the moist hearth-baked breads of Connaught (this is where, occasionally, you may find corned beef).

The bountiful Irish table includes roast meats accompanied by sauces of bread or onions, thin gravies that taste wholly of meat, and stuffings of sausage, apple, and sage; whole salmon are brought "leppin' fresh" from the dockside to the table, troubled by little more than steam and homemade mayonnaise; lobsters, oysters, and Dublin Bay prawns, which grow succulently sweet in our cold seawater, are served with drawn butter or a light sauce made of cream, not flour.

Turkeys with a delightfully gamy savor are accompanied by lardons of smoky bacon, chickens that actually taste like chicken, and flocks of game birds, from squab, quail, and pheasant, to woodcock, grouse, and snipe, are roasted with a huntsman's skill and served alongside their roasted organs spread on a bit of buttery toast, with floury potatoes cooked multiple ways. Like most Western cultures, the Irish are not vegetarians, but they indulge their passion for meat with a distinct respect for its origins. Poultry at the butcher comes with head and feet still attached, and often even plastic-wrapped supermarket chickens are not entirely denuded of their feathers.

Irish stews include far more variations than the simple classic of mutton, potatoes, carrots, and onions. My father produced an excellent and unusual version of Irish stew from his mother's recipe that included small fluffy dumplings made of suet, flour, raisins, and parsley, that not only lightened the stew, but also stretched it, perhaps invented for large hungry families on Dublin's northside. My County Mayo grandmother, however, on the opposite side of the country, had the bounty of a rural area at her fingertips, and her stew was thickened with nothing more than potatoes and onions cooked until they almost fell apart.

Irish vegetable dishes are legendary, especially colcannon, the traditional autumn dish of mashed potatoes and chopped kale (not cabbage, as occasionally seen when colcannon is made in the United States), served in a high mound filled with a pool of melted butter so each forkful can be dipped into the butter. It wouldn't be Halloween night (Samhain, in the Irish language) without a heaping plateful of colcannon, to keep the chill and the ghostly spirits away, followed by a thick slice of barmbrack, or simply brack, a sweetened yeast bread filled with dried fruits. Each glistening dark-brown loaf contains a toy ring or a coin, carefully wrapped in paper, to bring luck to the recipient for the coming year.

But brack (from the Irish word "breac," meaning cake, or loaf) barely scratches the surface of Irish baking. Every region makes brown bread in a different style, but the classics usually contain little more than wholemeal flour, baking soda (or "bread soda," as we call it), salt, and buttermilk. The skill is in the mixing, with the hands of the experienced cook feeling exactly how much liquid and how much kneading are required for the moistest, most delicately flavored loaf. Traditionally, brown bread was cooked in a pot-oven or a "bastible," a cast-iron, three-legged pot set into the fire, covered, and heaped with glowing coals. The resulting bread was moist with a faint, almost indefinable hint of turf smoke. (One of my elderly great-uncles in County Meath, who lived in an old thatched cottage, baked in a bastible until the end of his life, in the 1960's, sucking gently on a pipe while he waited the requisite hour for his bread to finish baking.)

Punch's Green Ribbon Tea
Capital
AMOND BAND TEA
Capital
Save this coupon
113 gms
Twining Crosfield & Co. (Ireland) Ltd., 45 Marrowbone Lane, Dublin, 8.
Quality Tested
Punch's Green Ribbon Tea
43p
BARRY'S TEA 43p
Brooke Bond
1/6
DIVIDEND TEA
1/4 LB. NET
DIVIDEND TEA
1/8
1/4 lb. net
MUSGRAVE
Brooke Bond
1/6
MUSGRAVE
Brooke Bond
1/6

# STOCKING THE IRISH KITCHEN IN AMERICA

## Pantry Basics

You'll need some basic ingredients in your pantry to make your kitchen authentically Irish, and you'll also find notes here on swapping in American ingredients for Irish ones for the best results.

## Dairy

Irish butter is cultured, meaning the cream is treated with a culture before it is churned. The resulting butter has more complexity and depth of flavor. You can culture and churn your own cream quite easily at home with the help of a little buttermilk and a food processor, but what's a little harder to match is the significantly higher butterfat of our butter and cream, which makes for a much thicker, more unctuous product. We tend to like our dairy in full-fat mode; skim and lower-fat milk is not always readily available. For most of these recipes, unless otherwise stated, use whole milk.

## Flours

The Irish distinguish between "plain flour," which is mostly like American all-purpose flour, and "cream flour," which is made from softer wheat. The best substitute for cream flour is a soft Southern flour such as Lily White, made from lower-protein wheat. Irish extra coarse wholemeal flour is what's typically used for brown breads and scones. No American flours are really as coarse as our extra coarse wholemeal, but a stoneground flour is your best bet, such as Arrowhead Mills, supplemented with some extra wheat bran and wheat germ.

## Sugars

In general, Irish sugar has a very coarse crystal. Irish sugar used to be made from sugar beets, not cane, but there is no appreciable taste difference. Our caster sugar has a finer crystal; the name comes from the fact that this finer sugar could go into a "caster," or sugar shaker. Caster sugar is the closest to American style sugar, but any white sugar is interchangeable, unless you're using it as a decoration to top baked goods. In that case, you'd need a large-crystal decorating sugar to sprinkle on top of buns or cakes to get similar results to Irish sugar. The Irish don't use much brown sugar. Golden demerara sugar is a cane sugar, unrefined so it retains the natural brown color of the dark cane syrup. It's unlike American light and dark brown sugar, which get their color from molasses added back to white sugar. Turbinado sugar is nearly the same, but you can substitute light brown for demerara.

## Meats

The Irish eat a lot of pork and a lot of lamb. We have good grass-fed beef, but it's not our number one meat the way it is in the United States. While a good grilled steak is always appreciated, beef is more typically seen in hearty stews such as Beef and Guinness, or savory pies, like the perennially popular Steak and Kidney (frequently called Snake and Pygmy). We eat far more lamb than Americans do, lamb chops and roast legs, ground lamb and lamb kidneys. Australian and New Zealand lamb is widely available in US markets, but I've been

finding that homegrown American lamb often tastes much better (less shipping?) and is less expensive.

## Fruits

Apple varieties can vary widely from country to country, and Ireland is deeply enamored of one particular baking apple, the Bramley, a big, lumpy, misshapen green apple that is perfect for tarts or desserts. It softens beautifully without becoming mushy, and it's very, very tart, able to stand up well to sweetening without losing its character. The best substitute that's widely available in the United States is probably a Granny Smith.

Berries grow beautifully in the cool, damp climate of Ireland, and Irish-grown strawberries are eagerly sought out in summer. They're smaller and naturally sweeter than the big fat California strawberries that are readily available in US grocery stores. Raspberries, red and gold, grow extremely well and plentifully, so they turn up on a lot of dessert tables, almost always served fresh, and usually with cream.

## Vegetables

We eat a lot of root vegetables: carrots, onions, turnips, rutabagas, and of course, the potato. But Irish potatoes tend to be very different from American ones—we don't like waxy potatoes and even a popular spud like the Yukon gold is a little too smooth. In Ireland, the most prized attribute is "flouriness," and the highest compliment is to say a batch of potatoes are "balls of flour." Instead of Irish varietals

Brown sodas at the English Market in Cork

like Roosters, Queens, Kerr Pinks, and Golden Wonders, look for American russets and baking potatoes. And then boil them!

## Styles of Bread

In Ireland, breads tend to be divided between soda bread and yeast-raised, often called pan. A soda is a round quick bread, brown or white, and raised with buttermilk and baking soda, whereas a pan is, as you might expect, a rectangularly sliced, yeast-raised loaf that was shaped and baked in a loaf pan. It's very similar to any American package loaf bread, although pans in Ireland don't have so much added sugar. Granary bread is a multigrain pan. Then there's batch, yeast-raised bread that's denser and chewier than pan. It's not baked in a loaf pan, but gets its name because the oblong loaves are baked pressed together, in a batch,

so they rise high and then they're pulled apart, leaving the sides pale, while the top crust is a dark brown. It's the best bread for toasting.

Wholemeal breads are sodas, but are a somewhat newer sub-category. The ingredients are the same as in a brown soda, but rather than being a round loaf marked with a cross, these commercially produced breads are baked in small, flat rectangles. They're extremely moist and deeply nutty, with an unusual aroma that arises from the added wheat bran and germ. McCambridge's is a particularly popular brand, and it will last a day or two longer than a traditional brown soda. These flat wholemeal loaves, which I call Moist Brown Bread (p. 188), are wonderful with smoked salmon or served sliced and buttered to accompany soups.

# SOURCES

## Where to Find Irish Food and Ingredients

If you live in a major metropolitan area in the Northeast—Boston, say, or New York City—finding authentic Irish food is pretty easy. You may have to make a few phone calls, but within easy reach you can find numerous shops and importers selling all manner of Irish teas, biscuits, and sausages, even household supplies. In traditionally Irish neighborhoods such as Woodside, Queens, in New York, you'll even find butchers making fresh Irish sausages and curing their own rashers and boiling bacon, as well as bakeries producing Irish baked goods.

Some authentic Irish products are now easily found in supermarkets all across the United States, so you can get Kerrygold butter, salted (in the gold wrapper) and unsalted (in the silver wrapper), which is the brand I always eat at home. Wherever you find Kerrygold, you'll usually also get Dubliner, a sharp cheese with the classic crumbly, fudgy texture of the best cheddars.

Failing that, you can order a lot of Irish food online.

## Food Ireland

This is one of the best all-around sites for basic ingredients, not just processed foods. Here's where you will find Irish flours, such as Odlum's cream flour, a popular brand of soft wheat flour for baking, as well as Odlum's Extra Coarse Wholemeal, the flour that gives brown soda bread its distinctly nutty flavor. You can also order meats, beverages, sweets and jams, and even fresh baked goods.

www.foodireland.com

## Good Food Ireland

An Irish-based website, Good Food Ireland exists to promote excellent Irish food and producers, and it's packed with information on the top purveyors of different types of food. If you click on the link "Buy Online," it will take you to pages and pages of sites where you can buy foods directly from individual producers, many of whom have the capability to ship outside of Ireland. One such producer is the Burren Smokehouse (www.burrensmokehouse.ie), a wonderful artisan smoker of salmon and other fish.

It will take a little surfing, but there are lots of treasures to be discovered at Good Food Ireland's main site: www.goodfoodireland.ie.

## Little Shamrocks

The food section on this site has lots of non-perishable packaged items, such as Irish teas, jams and preserves, chocolates, biscuits and crackers, and mustards and other condiments.

www.littleshamrocks.com

## Jolly Grub

This site sells primarily British food, but they have a good section of commercial Irish foods, including the elusive red lemonade, a fizzy drink that's exclusive to Ireland, where it's a popular bar mixer. They also have frozen items such as sausages, rashers, black and white pudding, and soda bread.

www.jollygrub.com

## Irish Grub

Irish Grub is a California-based company that makes Irish style meats out of American pork, including rashers and sausages and black and white pudding. This is the place to get real boiling bacon.

www.irishgrub.com

## Schaller and Weber

So it's a German butcher. It's also the source of excellent pork products, including cured Irish boiling bacon. At their site, search "Irish" and you'll find it.

www.schallerweber.com

# BREAKFAST FOODS

## To Make a Savory Amblet

Take twelve yolks of new eggs, mix them very fine like a batter, some chives, parsley, a little grated nutmeg, pepper, and salt: put in your amblet pan a quarter of a pound of fresh butter melted, then put your compound in the pan over a slow fire till hardened.

—from an 18th century Irish cookbook manuscript

Breakfast in Ireland can be the best meal of the day. Staying at an Irish B&B can beguile you into spending longer at the breakfast table than you did at the dinner table, beginning with a bowl of porridge, often topped with cream and sugar, and sometimes an alluring shot of whiskey as well. Then the meal moves on to the full "fry," sometimes called a "fry-up," consisting of a fried egg, sausages, rashers, and black and white pudding.

Accompaniments may include a grilled tomato half and heap of little mushrooms fried in butter, as well as brown bread or toast, and more butter. There might be cooked kidneys with your meal as well, or kippers, the little smoked herring that are so savory in the morning, and, in seaside communities, perhaps even a bit of fried fish, fresh caught. It was once common to finish the plate with a slice of bread cut in two triangles and fried in the oil remaining in the pan. The beans you sometimes see alongside a fry are usually put there for lunch or supper, not breakfast, but some cafeterias and restaurants aren't picky about that—if you want beans at breakfast, you're welcome to them. (My family always liked a slice of fried plum pudding with our fry on St. Stephen's Day, the morning after Christmas.) Once you've consumed your fry, it's time to finish the pot of tea and perhaps nibble a little more brown bread or toast with butter and homemade marmalade or jam, if you're lucky.

A full fry is not a meal for the faint-hearted, nor is it best for those who plan to sit on a tour bus all day! But if you're headed off hiking, fishing, biking, or plowing a field, perhaps, it will hold you for many, many hours of activity.

As might be expected with a dish called "the fry," it starts with a generous glug of cooking oil in a frying pan to cook the sausages and the slices of pudding, both black and white. When cooking sausages in large quantities, some restaurants deep-fry them, resulting in sausages that are evenly golden brown all over their exteriors, the ends bursting out slightly from the oil's heat.

Our rashers are not the fatty bacon slices that Americans know; we would call those "streaky rashers" because they are streaked with fat. Instead, the usual breakfast rasher is a slice of back bacon, a meaty cut with a narrow rim of fat around the edge just to add flavor. It's cured in salt or brine but not necessarily smoked (freshly cured rashers are called "green rashers"). Rashers are frequently grilled—or broiled in an American oven—to just cook them through but not to brown them.

When your rashers are grilled and your sausages and pudding fried; when the tomato halves have been grilled alongside the rasher or had their cut side browned in the skillet, the mushrooms have been lightly browned in hot fat, and the cooked foods are staying warm in a dish; when the boiling water has just been poured over the tea leaves in the pot; the bread is sliced and ready, the butter in a dish on the table, and the milk in a jug nearby; when all that is done, then everything is set aside to wait while the egg is fried.

It is a free-range egg; that's a given. We don't love battery-raised chickens or eggs in Ireland, and it's not hard to find free-range eggs in most shops—the butcher is often a good source—with dark yellow yolks and, almost always, brown shells. (Yes, I know there's no taste difference whatsoever between eggs in brown shells and eggs in white shells, but brown-shelled eggs look, and therefore taste, right to me.) There should still be plenty of oil in the pan, including any fats the meats have given off while cooking.

Break the egg into the hot oil. The outer edges of the white will sizzle and crackle, may take on a browned crisp "cuff," as my English friend, Rust says (if you don't like eggs with a cuff, like Rust does, reduce the heat slightly). There's no lid on the pan to cook the egg's top, nor do we flip it: over-easy is not an egg order in Ireland. Instead, with the edge of the spatula, you used to lift the cooked meats from the pan, flick the hot oil in the pan carefully over the yolk, until it's lightly filmed in a pale haze of just-cooked white, like a swelling pearl, ready to be lifted onto that plate laden with so many good things.

And then breakfast is ready.

# BLACK PUDDING

People—not just the Irish—have been eating blood puddings for centuries, in cultures all around the world. No Irish fry is truly complete without at least a slice of black and a slice of white pudding. And it's not just for breakfast anymore. Talented Irish chefs have found ways to incorporate it into salads and main dishes. Black pudding recipes vary wildly throughout Ireland; some include barley, breadcrumbs, and flour, but oatmeal is the old-fashioned thickener. Be sure it's steel-cut or pinhead oatmeal, and cook it until just tender. Individual nubs of oats should be visible in the final product. Store-bought versions will always be made in sausage casings, unlike this recipe, packed into a loaf pan.

It is far easier to buy black pudding ready-made, and there are lots of artisan producers making truly worthy black versions. But if you're able to come into possession of fresh pig's blood, you'll be all set to make this recipe. And if not—well, you'll know precisely what a good black pudding should contain.

Makes about 3 pounds

4 cups fresh pig's blood
2½ teaspoons salt
1½ cups steel-cut (pinhead) oatmeal
2 cups finely diced pork fat (or beef suet), finely chopped
1 large yellow onion, finely chopped
1 cup milk
1½ teaspoons freshly ground black pepper
1 teaspoon ground allspice

1   Preheat the oven to 325 degrees F and grease 2 glass loaf pans. (If you don't have glass loaf pans, line metal loaf pans with parchment to keep the blood sausage from reacting with the metal and creating an off-flavor.) Stir 1 teaspoon of salt into the blood.

2   Bring 2½ cups water to a boil and stir in the oats. Simmer, stirring occasionally, for 15 minutes, until just tender, not mushy.

3   Pour the blood through a fine sieve into a large bowl to remove any lumps. Stir in the fat, onion, milk, pepper, allspice and remaining 1 1/2 teaspoons salt. Add the oatmeal and mix to combine. Divide the mixture between the loaf pans, cover with foil, and bake for 1 hour, until firm. Cool completely. Seal in plastic wrap and either freeze for extended use or store in the refrigerator for up to a week.

4   To serve, cut a slice about 1/2-inch thick off the loaf. Fry in butter or oil until the edges are slightly crisped and browned.

# Drisheen and Tripe

When I used to go to "Irish camp" in the Aran Islands in the summers—where hordes of teenagers were supposedly working on our Irish language skills but were in fact idling without much supervision and hoping to work up the courage to talk to the opposite sex—I first ate drisheen with the family where I boarded. This was rough-and-ready summer camp, and we were spread out among the islanders like so many refugees, sent out to classes in the morning, and left to roam the island or swim all afternoon before we attended a ceilidh every night and eagerly hoped to meet girls. The *bean an tí*, literally the "woman of the house," had a large pot of sheep's blood in a windowsill where it sat for a day or two until it was thick. Not surprisingly, we few teenagers boarding with her affected great disgust. Then she mixed it up with cream, a little oatmeal, and some leaves of tansy (a wild herb with a faintly minty flavor). She packed it into a mold and steamed it, then she sliced it, fried it, and fed it to us for breakfast with a fried egg and buttered toast. And all the complaining stopped. I was hooked—it was the most flavorful, delicate black pudding I'd ever eaten, a gustatory experience that stopped me in my tracks.

When packed into casings and sliced, black pudding is typically served in a rich cream sauce with long-cooked tripe. Drisheen and tripe is a Munster thing, more often seen in Counties Cork and Kerry than in the rest of Ireland. Because it's made with fewer thickeners and with cream for added fat, the finished sausage is pale and tender. The tansy, a yellow-flowering herb that was a powerful anti-parasitic, had a pleasantly sharp taste, keeping the richness from being cloying. It would be rare now to find drisheen flavored with tansy. These days it's usually replaced with a hint of fresh thyme or even a bit of mint.

# WHITE PUDDING

If you're not keen on the idea of black pudding, white pudding may be a good place to begin. It doesn't require any blood, but instead has rolled oats, lard, pork liver, and, in old-fashioned versions, "lights," or ground lungs. Lights are harder to find these days, so it's fine to leave it out. Good white pudding is quite spicy with white pepper and serves as a real foil to the richer black pudding that it always sits alongside on the plate. It's also easier to make at home. Again, it would be packed into sausage casings at a butcher shop, but for home cooks, you can pack it into loaf pans to cook it and slice before frying.

Makes about 3 pounds

4 cup rolled oats (not quick oats)
1¾ cups whole milk
½ pound pork liver
1 medium yellow onion, peeled and coarsely chopped
2 cups finely chopped pork fat
2 teaspoons salt
1 teaspoon white pepper
½ teaspoon dried thyme leaves, crushed
¼ teaspoon ground nutmeg

1   Put the oats and milk in a large bowl, cover, and leave to soak for at least 3 hours, or overnight.

2   Preheat the oven to 325 degrees F and grease two glass loaf pans. (If you don't have glass, line metal pan with parchment.)

3   Bring 4 cups of water to a boil in a large saucepan and add the liver and the chopped onion. Cook for 3 to 4 minutes until the liver is lightly poached and firm, and the onion is slightly softened. Drain and cool slightly.

4 Pulse the liver and onions with the pork fat, salt, pepper, thyme, and nutmeg in a food processor until chopped finely, but don't overprocess into a paste. Turn this mixture into the bowl with the oatmeal and stir to combine.

5 Divide the mixture between the loaf pans, cover with foil, and bake for 1 hour. Chill, seal with plastic wrap, and store in the refrigerator. To serve, fry a slice in butter or oil until lightly browned.

## Tips for Pudding Success

Not sure about the salt or spice in your black or white pudding? After mixing it together, but before baking, fry a tablespoon in butter or oil in a small skillet over medium heat until cooked through. Taste and adjust seasoning. You may want more salt, herbs, or white pepper—I like my white pudding very spicy with pepper but only a faint hint of nutmeg.

Baking it simply covered with foil will make a firm, drier pudding, ideal for storing and frying later, but if you want a slightly more tender texture, before baking, place the foil-covered loaf pans in a large roasting tin and pour hot water halfway up the sides of the pans. This improvised water bath keeps the puddings moister and the texture more delicate.

# IRISH SAUSAGES

Sausages are a constant throughout Irish society. They turn up at breakfast, lunch, and dinner, and they're served as cocktail food, late-night snacks, birthday party treats, and finger food. They're everywhere, in sizes large and small. And not only do we eat them with knife and fork on a plate, but we also pick them up in our fingers to dip into sauces, and a personal favorite, we slit them lengthwise and lay them on a slice of buttered toast, with a little mustard alongside, for the best breakfast sandwich I can think of.

Most people buy their sausages, which are typically about ¾ to 1 inch in diameter and about 4-inches long, but there is also a tradition of home sausage making, which doesn't involve casings. If you have a meat grinder or a grinding attachment on your stand mixer, this is the time to use it. Then you can use a pound of pork shoulder instead of starting with ground pork. Grind the meat twice for a really fine texture.

If you don't have a grinder, pulse the fat in the food processor until it's finely chopped, and then mix it with the ground meat and pulse again. You may be able to ask the butcher to grind the meat and fat together for you. Don't skimp on the fat—it's crucial.

Roll the sausage mixture into either fingers or patties and fry. They shouldn't really be at all spicy, but leaving out the spice will make them bland. After you've mixed them up, fry a tablespoon and taste to check the seasoning.

*Makes 12 sausages*

1 pound pork shoulder, cubed (or
    1 pound ground pork)
½ pound pork fat
¼ to ½ cup white breadcrumbs
1½ teaspoons salt
¼ to ½ teaspoon ground allspice
¼ teaspoon white pepper
¼ teaspoon dried sage, crushed

1   Grind the meat and fat with a grinder, or pulse the fat in the food processor until finely ground and then mix in the meat. Add the remaining ingredients and pulse, or grind again.

2   Form into 12 patties or fingers, and fry in oil or butter over medium heat until lightly browned and cooked through, 8 to 10 minutes.

# MUSHROOMS AND KIDNEYS

Toward the beginning of Ulysses, Leopold Bloom famously buys, fries, and eats a pork kidney, which gave "to his breath the faint tang of urine." It's not the way to sell kidneys to a larger audience, but then, James Joyce wasn't exactly a food writer. Bloom liked pork kidneys, which I find bigger and not as tender as lamb kidneys, my preferred breakfast organ meat. Lamb kidneys are firm-textured and slightly, appealingly, chewy, with a good meaty flavor. They're readily available at Irish butchers and very inexpensive, but they need to be very fresh. You have to peel the membrane off the outside of each kidney, then cut each piece in half crossways, and peel or snip off any fat or sinew you find inside. Then you're ready to go. For a milder flavor, soak them in milk for 20 minutes before cooking. If you do, pat them well dry. Kidneys need high heat so they can brown quickly without a lot of moisture leaking out. Cooking them with onions and mushrooms is common, but I prefer the slightly tangier taste of shallot. Hot buttered toast is the ideal accompaniment.

*Makes 2 servings*

4 tablespoons butter

4 fresh lamb kidneys (6 to 8 ounces), cleaned and sliced
  as explained above

1 small shallot, finely minced

1 cup small white button mushrooms, cleaned and quartered

Salt and black pepper

1   Heat a cast-iron skillet over medium-high heat for 2 to 3 minutes, then add half the butter. Drop in the kidneys on top of the butter as it melts and sizzles. Cook 3 to 4 minutes, turning them halfway through, until the edges are browned. Remove to a warm dish.

2   Put the remaining butter in the pan and add the shallot and mushrooms. Cook 4 to 5 minutes until the mushrooms are browned and the shallot is softened. (This is a good time to make and butter your toast.)

3   Return the kidneys to the pan just to heat through, and season with salt and pepper.

# POTATO CAKES

When I was growing up, my dad made potato cakes as a way to use up leftover mashed potatoes and to try to stave off the hunger of four unfillable teenage boys. With a fried egg, rashers, and sausages, potato cakes made a breakfast that would stick to the ribs all morning. Nowadays, I make mashed potatoes simply in order to have potato cakes. I enjoy them so much, I've even cut them into smaller triangles and served them as a cocktail party nibble alongside sour cream flavored with chives for dipping. If you're using leftover mashed potatoes, remember these cakes work best with mashed potatoes that aren't too heavy with butter, milk, or cream, so the finished cakes taste floury and potato-like.

Makes 4 servings (basic proportions can be doubled, tripled, etc.)

2 cups leftover mashed potatoes
¾ to 1 cup all-purpose flour
1 teaspoon salt
¼ cup (½ stick) butter

1   Combine the potatoes with the flour and salt, mixing well with your hands, and knead on a lightly floured surface into a smooth dough, adding a little more flour if necessary to stop the dough from being sticky.

2   Divide the dough into quarters. On a lightly floured surface, use your hands to press each quarter into a circle about ½-inch thick and 6 inches in diameter.

3   In a cast-iron skillet over medium heat, melt 1 tablespoon of butter until sizzling but not brown. Slip in 1 cake and fry for 2 to 3 minutes, then flip and fry until browned, another 2 to 3 minutes. Remove to a plate. Repeat for the remaining cakes, adding a tablespoon of butter for each cake.

4   Serve immediately or hold in a 250 degree F oven for up to an hour before serving. Best slathered with yet more butter and lightly sprinkled with salt. Potato cakes can also be stored in the refrigerator for several days and reheated briefly on each side in a hot dry cast-iron skillet.

# PORRIDGE WITH CREAM

We love oats in Ireland; they're an ancient food, and the scholarly monks who once inhabited all the ruined abbeys that still dot this island regularly ate oats with milk or cream: it must be brain food. Pinhead oatmeal is what we call those tough little nubs of oats that you can buy in cans in Ireland and often in upmarket grocery stores in the United States. If you've merely boiled it according to package instructions and been unimpressed, try it the old-fashioned Irish way: Soak it overnight. For an even more tender porridge, I like to bring it to a boil in a saucepan, cover it, and let it sit on the back of the stovetop overnight. In the morning, you merely have to heat the porridge through, and it's ready to eat, no tedious half hour of simmering.

If you use this technique with traditional rolled oats (never quick or instant oats), you'll get creamy porridge. The top Irish brand is Flahavan's Progress Oatlets, and the oats are bigger and wider than America's Quaker Oats. But whatever oats you use, ensure creaminess by substituting milk for some or all of the water when cooking porridge. In Ireland, we often take our porridge with a dash of cream, a sprinkle of brown sugar—and, on special occasions, a tablespoon or two of whiskey.

*Makes 4 servings*
**1 cup pinhead oatmeal**
**3 cups water**
**¼ teaspoon salt**

1   Before you go to bed, put the oats, water, and salt in a heavy saucepan with a lid.

2   Bring to a boil, then turn off the heat, cover, and let the pan sit on the stovetop all night. It's not necessary to refrigerate.

3   In the morning, when you're ready to eat, stir up the oats. They will have absorbed all the water and the mixture will be thickened and stiff. Cook over medium heat, stirring vigorously and pressing any lumps against the side to break them up, just until hot throughout. Eat at once.

# THE VEGETARIAN FRY

Okay, so Ireland likes a meaty breakfast. What do vegetarians do? There are options besides resorting to a bowl of porridge every morning, and one of my favorites is to simply surround a fluffy mound of scrambled eggs with the usual accompaniments of grilled tomatoes and fried mushrooms. Using a little cream in the scrambled eggs makes them particularly unctuous. Add the requisite slice of brown bread and butter, and you have a meal even a confirmed meat-lover will enjoy.

For 1 serving
2 tablespoons butter
¾ cup white button mushrooms, thinly sliced
Salt and pepper
1 medium tomato, halved around the equator
2 eggs
2 tablespoons cream

1 Put one tablespoon of the butter in a skillet over medium-high heat and as soon as it sizzles, add the mushrooms. Sprinkle with salt and pepper and cook, stirring often, until the mushrooms are golden brown on the edges, about 5 minutes. If the heat is higher, the liquid the mushrooms give off will evaporate quickly and you can brown them faster. While the mushrooms cook, put the two tomato halves cut-side down in the skillet and let them soften and brown slightly.

2 Put the mushrooms and tomatoes aside on a serving plate and keep warm. Beat the eggs lightly in a cup with the cream. Add the remaining tablespoon of butter to the same skillet and melt the butter over medium heat. As soon as it sizzles, pour in the eggs and cook, turning them with a wooden spoon or, for fluffier eggs, a heatproof silicone spatula, until just set and not too dry, 2 to 3 minutes. Season with salt and pepper and spoon onto the plate with the mushrooms and tomatoes. Serve at once.

## Buttered Eggs

When hens are laying constantly in the summer, it's hard to believe you could ever be without eggs. But winter will come and with it, a dearth of eggs. Frugal Irish farm families in times past knew what to do when the eggs were flowing and the cows were giving milk freely, too: butter the eggs. It's best practiced on eggs that are literally still warm from being laid. A very thin layer of butter is rubbed around the egg, sealing it airtight and preserving it for several months. Eggshells are so porous the buttery flavor permeates the egg, which is why eggs are still buttered today rather than merely refrigerated.

## To make Buttered Eggs

To prepare your own buttered eggs, it is essential to have freshly laid eggs from directly underneath a hen. The eggs must still be warm or the preservation process won't work. A warm new-laid egg still has a slightly porous shell, so the softened butter is able to permeate the shell and completely seal it from oxygen. Use salted butter for best results.

To butter eggs, have butter at room temperature and rub it gently but completely into each warm egg using your hands. Be sure to really massage it into each egg for best results, using your hands to gently smooth off the excess butter and transfer it to the next egg. Store the eggs in regular egg cartons in a very cool place (the cellar of your Irish cottage is ideal). Buttered eggs keep for up to six months.

## To cook Buttered Eggs

You can use a buttered egg for any recipe that calls for eggs. If you simply cook the egg for breakfast, you may be pleased to find that it has a pronounced buttery taste. For some cooks, however, the term "buttered eggs" refers to a method of scrambling eggs that makes them custard-like. Don't add water or milk, just butter. These are pure luxury.

To make 3 to 4 servings
**6 buttered eggs (or regular eggs)**
**3 tablespoons unsalted butter**
**Salt and pepper**

1. Break the eggs into a bowl and beat well with a fork or whisk. Heat a nonstick or cast-iron pan over low heat and melt the butter in it.

2. Pour in the eggs and cook, turning over gently with a heatproof spatula and keeping the heat very low, until just barely set. The eggs should still be slightly wet. Sprinkle lightly with salt and pepper. Eat at once.

# FRIED FRESH WHITEFISH

Some of the best fish I ever ate for breakfast came after the first night I ever ate at the renowned Ballymaloe House in County Cork. We were staying at a very casual bed and breakfast in nearby Ballycotton—so casual that, when we came back after dinner with some friends who'd driven to meet us for dinner and decided to stay over instead of driving on, we booked them in ourselves, found a key to an unoccupied bedroom hanging on a shelf in the entry, and showed them to their room ourselves.

In the morning, the lady of the house calmly welcomed her unexpected new guests in the breakfast room and said to us all, "I've not much in the place to give you this morning for breakfast. You can have porridge or I'll do you a fry, or, if you don't mind waiting a moment, I'll cook up a bit of that fish that himself is after unloading down on the dock this minute. He was out all night." She nodded toward the window as she spoke, and we turned to see her husband unloading big wooden crates of fish from a fishing boat alongside the small dock below the house.

After the night's feast at Ballymaloe, we'd all sworn we'd never eat again. But when she reappeared with a platter of big thick chunks of haddock, the edges golden brown and crisp, we fell on it like starving people. It was moist, meaty, and tender, some of the freshest fish I'd ever had the pleasure of eating. And while my average hunk of fried fish isn't as good most days, it still evokes that memorable meal.

*Makes 4 servings*

1½ pounds fresh whitefish fillets, such as haddock or cod, each fillet about ½-inch thick
1 teaspoon salt
¼ cup flour
3 tablespoons butter
Lemon wedges

1 Sprinkle the fish on both sides with salt and flour. Heat the butter in a large skillet over medium-high heat until it sizzles.

2 Lay the floured fish into the butter and fry for 2 to 3 minutes on each side, until the edges are crisp and golden brown and the fish is cooked through. Eat at once, with lemon wedges on the side for each diner to squeeze over the fish.

## Larded Onions

Peel your onions and boil them very slow for a qr of an hour lard them and put them into a small crock with melted butter, pepper and salt, bake them in a smart oven the crock must not be covered half an hour is enough drain them from the oil, put some good gravy under them and serve them up.

—from an 18th century Irish cookbook manuscript

Traditionally, the Irish aren't big snackers. As an agrarian society, the day was punctuated by a large breakfast, a big midday dinner, and a lighter evening supper, or "tea," as the evening meal is still known in many homes. Add in the religious element with its various times for fasting and strictures on what could be eaten during which times, and you get some pretty strong food habits that do not include a lot of eating outside of mealtimes. Times have changed, certainly; when I was a child, we were never given food when it wasn't mealtime, whereas my own children sometimes seem to have more snacks than meals! And yet, there are smaller bites that are traditionally Irish, whether they form the basis of a light meal or a hasty nibble before going out to the pub or after coming home. Some, such as Potted Shrimp, can also serve as an elegant starter to a heavier meal, perhaps served with toast points; but if you slather it on a thick slab of buttered bread, it's a great midnight snack. In general, however, we like our sandwiches simple and thin. They're no less savory and delicious for that.

# POTTED SHRIMP

"Potting" fish or meats was an old way of storing them. Leftover meats such as chicken or ham or seafood such as fish or shrimp were pounded together with nearly an equal quantity of butter (I use a little less) to make a rough paste, then seasoned with salt and mace, nutmeg, or another warm spice. The paste was then poured into a small container and covered with clarified butter, sealing out the air so it could be stored in a cool pantry. Because it's now stored in the refrigerator, I don't bother to clarify the butter—the milk solids don't bother me or affect the flavor. And I don't "pound" it but simply run it through the food processor. (Some recipes use tiny shrimp and leave them whole in the butter.) The lemon juice is not traditional, but it ties all the flavors together well. Served on crisp, hot thin toast or with crackers or bread, it's an excellent light lunch, a starter, or even a savory at the end of a meal.

Makes about 3 cups

½ cup (1 stick) butter, plus ¼ cup (½ stick) melted butter (or a little more as needed)
8 ounces medium raw shrimp, peeled (about 2 cups)
1 tablespoon lemon juice
⅛ teaspoon freshly grated nutmeg
Salt and pepper

1   In a large skillet over medium-low heat, melt the ½ cup of butter. Add the shrimp and increase the heat slightly. Cook, stirring frequently, just until the shrimp is pink and opaque, 3 to 4 minutes. Do not overcook or the shrimp will be tough and rubbery.

2   Turn the shrimp into a food processor. Add the lemon juice and nutmeg and a sprinkle of salt and pepper. Process to form a coarse paste. Taste and add salt or lemon juice if needed.

3   Divide the shrimp paste among 2 or 3 ramekins or small bowls (or one larger dish, but smaller ones are more common) and smooth the surface with the back of a spoon. Pour the remaining melted butter over the top of each to make an even layer that seals the entire surface. Store in the refrigerator for up to a week.

## Potted Salmon

Substitute 2 cups cooked, skinless, boneless wild salmon for the shrimp

## Potted Chicken

Substitute 2 cups cooked, skinless, boneless chicken breast for the shrimp, leave out the lemon juice, and season the mixture with ground mace instead of nutmeg.

## Potted Ham

Substitute 2 cups cooked, cubed ham for the shrimp, leave out the lemon juice, and season the mixture with ground mace instead of nutmeg.

# CRUBEENS (PIGS' FEET)

Pigs' feet, boiled with aromatics, were a hand food, perhaps to be eaten out of hand during a day at the horse races or at a country fair. They were a specialty food that turned up at public events and special occasions, not necessarily something that was a regular staple in shops. They're sticky and unctuous, and you nibble the bits of tender, succulent meat off the bone. Pork is so widely eaten in Ireland that pigs' trotters are readily available at butcher shops.

8 pigs' trotters
2 medium yellow onions
1 large carrot
2 tablespoons kosher salt (or 1 tablespoon table salt)
3 to 4 sprigs fresh thyme
½ teaspoon whole black peppercorns
10 whole cloves

1   Put all the ingredients in a large, heavy stewpot and cover with water. Bring to a boil over high heat. Reduce to medium and simmer gently, loosely covered for 3 to 4 hours until the meat is completely tender. Cool slightly and serve just warm enough to handle.

# PICKLED ONIONS

If you're eating a cheese sandwich and something seems to be missing . . . it's probably that you need a pickled onion or two alongside. Back in the old days, there wasn't that much food in Irish pubs, but in country pubs you might see a jar or bowl of pickled onions, and you could have one free with your pint. Salty and tangy, it's just a savory little bite that sort of whets your appetite. They were considered to be packed with vitamins, and the vinegar was thought to help digestion. Salting the onions first helps keep them crisp. (If you don't have pickling salt, you can use kosher, but be sure it's the kind without additives like anti-caking agents.)

Makes 2 cups

½ cup pickling salt
1 pound pearl onions (about 2 cups), trimmed and peeled
2 cups white vinegar
3 tablespoons sugar
12 whole black peppercorns
1 bay leaf

1  Put 3 cups of water in a medium glass or ceramic bowl (not metal) and stir in the salt to dissolve. Add the onions and lay a small plate on top to hold them underwater. Leave them for 2 days. Drain and rinse them.

2  In a medium saucepan over medium heat, boil the vinegar, sugar and peppercorns. Set aside to cool.

3  Pack the onions into a glass jar (because of their size, you may need a quart jar to hold them). Add the bay leaf, pour on the vinegar, and cover the jar. Refrigerate at least 2 weeks before eating them. The onions will last for several months.

# DEVILLED CRAB

Irish crab is excellent. Stone crabs in particular taste deeply "crabby." They tend to be very large, and they're fresh, sweet, briny, meaty, and packed with flavor. "Devilling" foods is an old tradition in the British Isles, a sort of creamy and mustard-sharp treatment that piques your taste buds and heightens the natural sweetness of the food. Devilled crab is often served in the cleaned shells, but it's just as good in individual ramekins or a shallow single casserole.

Serves 4

For the devilled crab:

½ cup heavy cream
½ cup chopped parsley
1 stalk celery, finely chopped
2 scallions, thinly sliced
1½ teaspoons dry mustard powder
1 teaspoon salt
1½ pounds crabmeat

For the topping:

½ cup breadcrumbs
¼ cup (½ stick) butter, melted

1   Preheat oven to 350 degrees F and butter 48-ounce ramekins or a shallow 1-quart casserole.

2   Combine all the devilled crab ingredients but the crab in a mixing bowl, tossing well to combine.

3   Gently turn the crabmeat into the mixture, folding just to combine but being careful not to break up the chunks of meat too much.

4   Divide the mixture among the prepared ramekins or spread it in the casserole. Sprinkle with breadcrumbs and drizzle with the melted butter. Bake for 25 minutes, until bubbling and browned. Serve hot.

# SANDWICHES

Irish sandwiches tend to be quite thin by American standards. In general, we don't like hugely overstuffed sandwiches, preferring thin and savory fillings on thin-sliced bread. The difference is, we eat a lot of them at once! Here are some standard Irish sandwich fillings, to be made on white, brown or granary (multigrain) pans (or sliced commercial loaves). The bread is usually buttered first and nearly all sandwiches are cut diagonally into two triangles, never two rectangles.

## Egg Mayonnaise

Mash four hardboiled eggs with the back of a fork and stir in 1/4 cup mayonnaise, 1 tablespoon chopped chives (or finely minced scallion), and season with salt and pepper.

## Cheese 'n' Onion Sandwiches

Layer onto buttered white bread 1/4-inch slices of white cheddar, a few thin slices of ripe tomato, and just enough onion, cut into paper-thin rings, for flavor.

## Tuna and Sweet Corn

Drain a 6-ounce can of tuna and mix with 3 tablespoons mayonnaise and 1/4 cup of drained canned corn. Spread on buttered brown pan. Sometimes the tuna is topped with a layer of coleslaw made with cabbage, shredded carrot, and mayonnaise—this is surprisingly delicious.

## The Chip Butty

I can't claim I was deeply into this sandwich, but it's enduringly popular, particularly after an evening in the pub: Butter two slices of white pan and line one with a row of thick-cut French fries (the "chips"). Top with ketchup or brown sauce, as desired. Then with the other slice of buttered bread, crush together, and eat without cutting.

# FARMHOUSE VEGETABLE SOUP

The "farmhouse" part of the title has become inseparable from "vegetable soup," but it does conjure up images of a hearty pot of wholesome soup on the back of the range in a farm kitchen. Farmhouse vegetable soup also tends to be mostly puréed, with just a few chunks of visible vegetable left floating. And it's often enriched with a dash of heavy cream, but it's no problem to leave that out. I love this simple soup with crunchy, freshly made croutons floating on the surface. They only take a few moments to prepare.

Makes 4 to 6 servings

2 tablespoons butter
2 medium yellow onions, chopped
3 stalks celery, thinly sliced
4 large russet potatoes, peeled and diced
2 large carrots, diced
2 quarts (8 cups) chicken stock
1 teaspoon fresh thyme leaves
½ teaspoon dried sage
1 cup frozen peas
¼ cup heavy cream (optional)
Salt and pepper

Croutons for serving:

2 thick slices good bakery bread
3 tablespoons olive oil

1   Heat the butter in a large, heavy soup pot over medium heat. Stir in the onions and celery, and put the lid on the pot. Cook the vegetables covered for 6 to 7 minutes, so they steam and soften but do not brown.

2   Add the potatoes, carrots, stock, thyme, and sage. Bring to a boil, cover loosely, and simmer for 20 to 25 minutes, until all the vegetables are tender. Add the peas for the last 5 minutes of cooking time.

3   Add the cream, if using, and season to taste with salt and pepper. Using an immersion blender, purée most of the soup, leaving a few visible chunks of vegetables.

4   To serve, cut the crusts off the bread and trim the slices into 1/2-inch cubes. Heat the oil in a nonstick skillet over medium heat, add the bread, and fry briskly, shaking the pan and turning the croutons, until golden brown, 3 to 4 minutes. Spoon the soup into bowls and sprinkle with croutons.

# CELERY SOUP

We love celery in Ireland, and I ate a lot of it growing up. Funny enough, almost never in the raw form, as in celery sticks, but always cooked in soups and stews, and also cooked in thick slices until tender and tossed in a buttery cream sauce as a side dish. My American wife had almost the opposite experience: she mostly ate it raw, in salads or with tuna, perhaps stuffed with peanut butter, so she was surprised to see how often it showed up on Irish tables as a cooked side dish. Celery's delicate, sweet flavor makes a wonderful soup.

*Makes 6 servings*
¼ cup (½ stick) butter
1 head celery (about 1 pound), trimmed and sliced thin
2 large russet potatoes, peeled and diced
2 medium yellow onions, chopped
2 quarts (8 cups) chicken stock
1 bay leaf
¼ teaspoon ground nutmeg
1 cup light cream
Salt and pepper

1   Melt the butter in a large, heavy soup pot over medium heat. Stir in the celery, potatoes, and onion, and cover the pot. Cook for 6 to 7 minutes, to soften the vegetables without browning them.

2   Add the stock, bay leaf, and nutmeg. Bring to a boil, reduce heat, and simmer gently for 20 to 25 minutes, until the vegetables are completely tender. Remove the bay leaf, and with an immersion blender, purée the soup until completely smooth. Stir in the cream, heat through, and season to taste with salt and pepper.

# LEEK AND POTATO SOUP

This soup shows up on menu after menu, because it features two favorite Irish vegetables. On its own, a plain potato soup has the potential to be sort of heavy and bland. Add flavorful leeks with their vaguely squeaky texture between the teeth, and the soup lightens up and takes on character. Be sure to wash the leeks after slicing so you get out any dirt hiding between the layers.

*Makes 6 servings*

¼ cup (½ stick) butter
6 large russet potatoes
2 to 3 leeks, trimmed, white and green parts sliced, and well washed
2 quarts (8 cups) chicken stock
2 cups light cream (or whole milk)
Salt and pepper

1   Melt the butter in a large, heavy soup pot over medium heat. Stir in the potatoes and leeks, and cover the pot. Cook for 6 to 7 minutes, to soften the vegetables without browning them.

2   Add the stock, bring to a boil, reduce heat, and simmer for 25 to 30 minutes, until the potatoes are completely tender and falling apart to thicken the soup.

3   Stir in the cream or milk, heat through, and season to taste with salt and pepper. If you like, you can eat this soup as is, with thinner broth and chunks of vegetables, or puree it partially, or purée it into a smooth cream. It's good whatever you do.

# CREAM OF NETTLE SOUP

Two of my brothers were prone to eczema, so my mother used to take them to see the local "bonesetter," as neighborhood healers were known. Some bonesetters in Ireland were truly famous for their healing powers, and it's a fine tradition that modern science has not completely killed off, especially in the country. That's because a lot of bonesetters know exactly what they're doing when it comes to herbal treatments, and this soup is a prime example. Not only did my two brothers have to eat it, we all had it as a sort of spring tonic. It cleared up their skin and made us all feel sprightly. Now I don't eat it for health but only as a foraging gourmet, because nettles have a terrific fresh green taste, reminiscent of spinach, but without tannic undertones. Wear gloves and long sleeves to collect and wash them. Once they hit the hot water, their stinging power is gone. Also, be sure to use the tender young shoots of early spring; later the stalks get tough.

Makes 4 servings

¼ cup (½ stick) butter
2 leeks, trimmed, sliced, and well washed
1 medium yellow onion, chopped
4 large russet potatoes, peeled and diced
2 quarts (8 cups) chicken stock
1 pound fresh nettles (pick when no higher than 12 inches), well rinsed
1 cup heavy cream, Greek yogurt, or crème fraîche (or more for serving)
Salt and pepper

1   In a large, heavy soup pot over medium heat, melt the butter and add the leek, onion, and potato. Stir to coat with the butter, then cover and cook 6 to 7 minutes to soften the vegetables without browning.

2   Add the stock and bring to a boil. While the soup is boiling, stir in the nettles by handfuls (don't forget your gloves!). They'll wilt, and you can add more.

3   When all the nettles have been added, reduce heat and simmer the soup for 25 to 30 minutes until the vegetables are completely tender.

4   Purée the soup using an immersion blender (or carefully, in batches, in a blender or food processor) until completely smooth. Stir in the cream, yogurt, or crème fraiche and season to taste with salt and pepper. If you like, swirl a little more of the dairy product on top of each bowl of soup.

## To Ragout a Breast of Veal

Cut a breast of veal in small pieces about two inches square season it with pepper and salt then fry it till it is half ready then put it into two quarts of green peas two or three onions half a pound of bacon cut as small as dice a bunch of sweet herbs cover it with small broth or boiling water let it still till it is tender and serve it up.

—from an 18th century Irish cookbook manuscript

The Irish excel at stews, and not just Irish stew. There are many variations that feature chunks of meat and tender vegetables in rich gravies. Some are highly regional, such as Coddle, a stew that is so closely identified with Dublin it's barely been heard of, much less eaten, in other parts of Ireland. Others, such as Beef in Guinness, are more modern but no less beloved and have developed over the years to take advantage of our obvious local ingredients. That's where seafood chowders come in: they are a big favorite, turning up all across the country, and usually each bowl is absolutely loaded with lots of varieties of seafood, chunks of fish, mussels, and prawns. And that's why it belongs in stews, not soups.

# CODDLE

On a Saturday night in Dublin, I'm told, back in the day, a pot of coddle could be found in kitchens all over town. It was made with sausages and rashers, onions and potatoes, and not much else. Carrots may show up in more modern variations, but they were emphatically not part of the original dish. The point of coddle was to stew it up earlier in the day, let it cool, and then reheat it after an evening in the pub, at the pictures, or at a dance—whatever the entertainment was that evening. Even now, I find coddle is a dish that tastes best reheated, which makes the gravy thick. It's hearty and filling all on its own, and the only traditional accompaniment might be one more glass of beer. Don't try to make this with American bacon, which is too fatty. If you don't have Irish rashers, try substituting Canadian bacon, which is also made from the back, not belly, of the pig. You can use the sausage meat on p. 34, but ideally you'll have sausages in casings so they can stew without breaking up. Using chicken stock and thyme leaves is a modern touch—real old-fashioned coddle is cooked in water and flavored with salt—but it's a mild-mannered improvement on an already good dish.

*Makes 6 servings*

2 large yellow onions, sliced into rings

6 large russet potatoes, peeled and sliced ¼-inch thick

2 pounds Irish sausages, in casings

1 pound rashers, preferably not smoked, rind discarded, rashers cut into 2-inch pieces

1 teaspoon fresh thyme leaves

Salt and pepper

6 cups chicken stock

2 tablespoons chopped fresh parsley

1  In a large stewpot, layer the onions, potatoes, sausages, and rasher pieces, sprinkling a little salt and pepper and a bit of the thyme over the potatoes in each layer.

2  Pour the chicken stock over everything. If you need a little more liquid to cover, add a cup or two of water. Bring to a boil, cover loosely, and simmer for 30 to 40 minutes, until the potatoes are tender.

3  Taste and adjust seasoning. Sprinkle with parsley and eat at once, or ideally, let cool and reheat in the evening or the next day, when the stew will have mellowed and thickened.

# BEEF AND GUINNESS STEW

My first job ever, at age 12, was in a pub in Ashbourne, County Meath, as what used to be called "pot boy" (the same job Pegeen Mike hires Christy, the "Playboy," to do in J.M. Synge's play "Playboy of the Western World"). Nowadays that same job is usually called "lounge boy," and it entails wiping tables and (until pretty recently) emptying ashtrays—not exactly glamorous then or now. But I loved it, and I was fascinated by an elderly couple who used to come in every day and drink two bottles of Guinness apiece, in total silence, without taking off their heavy coats, no matter what the weather. It was long believed in Ireland that bottled Guinness was particularly rich in iron, and it was drunk by pregnant women, invalids, and the elderly as a sort of cure-all.

Whether it has any health benefits (and modern medical science rather thinks not), bottled Guinness makes a warm and filling beef stew with a hint of a bitter undertone in the gravy. A touch of brown sugar tempers the stout, prevents the stew from tasting too heavy, and cuts through the richness of the buttery mashed potatoes. It's a perfect dish for a cold winter night. This makes a huge batch, partly because it reheats so beautifully; it's even better the second day.

*Makes 8 to 10 servings*

5 pounds stew beef, such as chuck, cut into 1½-inch cubes
½ cup all-purpose flour
Salt and freshly ground black pepper
5 tablespoons suet or vegetable oil
3 to 4 large yellow onions, coarsely chopped
1 pound white mushrooms, halved
2 12-ounce bottles Guinness Extra Stout
2 cups beef stock
1 teaspoon brown sugar
1 teaspoon dried thyme leaves
Generous pinch of nutmeg
4 bay leaves

1. In a large bowl, toss the meat, flour, and some salt and pepper, until the meat is coated.

2. Heat the suet or oil in a large Dutch oven or stewpot over high heat. When the fat is very hot, add the meat all at once and fry, stirring occasionally, until well browned, about 10 minutes. Remove the browned meat from the pot and set aside on a platter.

3. Add the onions to the same pot and cook over medium heat until they just become translucent, 3 to 4 minutes. Return the beef to the pot and add the mushrooms, stout, stock, sugar, thyme, nutmeg, and bay leaves. Add salt and pepper, using a light hand with the salt at this stage.

4. Bring to a boil, then reduce the heat, cover, and simmer gently for 2 hours. Stir occasionally.

Note: Bottled Is Best

Don't make this stew with canned pub draught Guinness. That type is great for drinking, but it's too bubbly for cooking. Use the bottled stuff, the old-fashioned way. It's a different brew altogether, the way Guinness used to taste, with a different alcohol content, different flavor, and none of those foamy bubbles you don't need in stew.

# FINGLAS IRISH STEW WITH DUMPLINGS

My father hails from Finglas, on the north side of Dublin, and he always made his Irish stew with dumplings in it. Even more interesting, the dumplings were dotted with fresh parsley and raisins. Sound like it's not authentic? My Dublin-born and -bred grandmother made it that way herself. Perhaps it's a subset of Irish stew recipes, but it's my family's subset and I love it. If the idea of dumplings goes against your sense of Irish stew, use the excellent recipe below and merely leave out the dumplings.

The important thing is to use good lean lamb chops. And always and only lamb—if it's not, it's not Irish stew. Some say keeping the bones in while cooking adds flavor; it's entirely up to you. My dad used beef suet in his dumplings but I tend to have butter around more than suet. I also commit the heresy of browning the meat lightly first. It tastes better to modern palates, and a lot of Irish people do it that way, but if you want truly authentic Irish stew, skip browning, layer un-floured meat with the vegetables, and use mutton stock (um, you know, if you have any lying around) or water instead of chicken stock.

Makes 6 to 8 servings
3 tablespoons flour
Salt and pepper
3 pounds large meaty lamb chops, cut into large pieces

3 tablespoons cooking oil
6 to 8 large russet potatoes, peeled and sliced
2 large yellow onions, sliced
2 large carrots, sliced
1 tablespoon fresh thyme leaves, chopped
2 quarts (8 cups) chicken stock or water

For the dumplings:
1½ cups all-purpose flour
1 teaspoon baking powder
½ teaspoon salt
½ cup butter (or half butter, half vegetable shortening)
2 tablespoons chopped, fresh parsley
2 tablespoons raisins (or golden raisins)
⅓ cup cold water

1   In a large bowl, combine the flour with ½ teaspoon salt and ¼ teaspoon pepper. Toss the lamb pieces in this mixture to coat.

2   In a large heavy stewpot or Dutch oven, heat the oil over medium-high heat and brown the meat very lightly, just to let it take a little color. Set the meat aside in the bowl that held the flour and turn off the heat.

3   In the bottom of the stewpot, lay down a layer of potatoes
    and a few pieces of carrot and onion. Sprinkle with a bit of salt
    and pepper and a little of the thyme, top with a good layer of
    the lightly browned lamb, and continue, layering the lamb and
    vegetables with salt and pepper and thyme leaves.

4   Carefully pour the chicken stock down the inside edge of the pot
    to keep from rearranging your careful layers. Bring the liquid to
    a boil over medium-high heat. Reduce the heat, cover the pot
    tightly, and simmer gently for half an hour. Remove the lid, skim
    off any gray scum that may have formed, and cover again.
    Cook for another 1½ hours, until the vegetables and meat are
    fork-tender.

5   Combine the dry ingredients for the dumplings and cut in the
    butter until the mixture resembles coarse crumbs. Stir in the
    parsley and raisins, then add the water and stir to make a stiff
    dough.

6   Be sure the liquid in the stewpot is bubbling over medium heat.
    (If your stew looks dry—if no bubbling gravy is visible—you
    may not have a tight-fitting lid on your pot. Add another cup or
    two of water or stock and bring it to a boil before adding the
    dumplings.) Drop the dumplings all over the surface of the stew
    by the heaping tablespoon. Cover with the lid and *do not lift* it for
    25 minutes. It's crucial to trap that steam and cook the dough. If
    you peek, the dumplings *will not rise*.

# BEEF AND OYSTER STEW

Just as oysters in America were once common food to fill up poor people, Ireland also has a long history with oysters being everyday rather than the luxury items they are now. So rather than the expensive dish this stew has become, adding oysters was once a way to stretch the more valuable beef. In fact, to make it more authentic, you could easily double the amount of oysters. It's a thick stew without a lot of sauce, which makes it easier to identify the oysters in the mix!

*Makes 6 servings*

**2 tablespoons all-purpose flour**
**Salt and pepper**
**1½ pounds stew beef or chuck, cut in 1½-inch pieces**
**2 tablespoons cooking oil**
**1 large yellow onion, diced**
**1 cup sliced white button mushrooms**
**1 12-ounce bottle Guinness Extra Stout**
**2 cups beef (or chicken) stock**
**2 tablespoons Worcestershire sauce**
**12 fresh shucked oysters, juices reserved (or 1 6-ounce can fresh oysters in their liquid)**

1  Put the flour in a shallow dish and toss it with ½ teaspoon salt and ¼ teaspoon pepper. Toss the beef in the flour to coat.

2  In a large, heavy stewpot or Dutch oven, heat the oil over medium-high heat and sear the beef, in batches if necessary, until nicely browned on all sides. Remove the beef and set it aside in the bowl that held the flour.

3  In the oil left in the pan, cook the onions and mushrooms over medium-high heat until softened and lightly browned, 7 to 8 minutes. Return the beef to the pan and add the Guinness, stock, and Worcestershire sauce.

4  Cover the pot tightly and simmer gently over medium heat for 1½ to 2 hours, until the beef is really tender and the gravy has thickened. At the end of cooking, add the oysters and their liquid and simmer for a couple of minutes, just to heat through and cook the oysters.

# BEEF AND BARLEY STEW

Barley is a key Irish grain: it's what we make Guinness from, and dark-roasted barley is what gives Guinness its color. If you've ever been in Dublin and smelled that sort of smoky, half-burnt aroma on the air, it's the wind blowing down the Liffey from the Guinness factory, carrying the scent of roasting barley across the city. An American guy I knew in Dublin once asked me, early in his tenure there, why he smelled so many fires all the time. When I sniffed the air and explained it was merely the Guinness factory, his face brightened and he said, "I kept wondering why that smell was making me hungry!" We say in Ireland about a hearty drink such as Guinness, "There's eating and drinking in it," but that also applies to this satisfying stew, containing a bottle of Guinness and thickened with barley.

*Makes 4 to 6 servings*

2 tablespoons cooking oil

1½ pounds stew beef or chuck, cut into 1½-inch pieces

Salt and pepper

1 large yellow onion, diced

2 large russet potatoes, peeled and diced

1 large carrot, diced

1 cup barley

6 cups beef or chicken stock

1 12-ounce bottle Guinness Extra Stout

2 tablespoons Worcestershire sauce

1 tablespoon light brown sugar

1 tablespoon fresh thyme leaves, chopped

2 bay leaves

1   Heat the oil in a large, heavy stewpot or Dutch oven over medium-high heat. Season the beef with salt and pepper, and sear, in batches if necessary, until the beef is nicely browned. Remove it from the pan to a dish and set aside.

2   In the oil and juices remaining in the pan, cook the onions until browned and tender, about 7 to 8 minutes, stirring often. Add all the remaining ingredients and stir to combine.

3   Bring the stew to a boil, then reduce heat, cover and simmer for 1½ to 2 hours until the meat, vegetables, and barley are very tender. Stir it once or twice during the cooking time, and if the stew seems dry, add another cup or two of water. At the end of cooking, taste and adjust the seasoning. With all that barley, you may need a little more salt.

# MONKFISH STEW WITH WHITE BEANS

This stew was my dad's masterpiece, both a standard suppertime fallback and a showstopping crowd-pleaser for guests. Is it a traditional, historic Irish dish? Well, I can guarantee no peasant was brewing it up in a thatched cottage, no matter how close it sat to the coastline. But it is real Irish food in that my extended family across Ireland and America enthusiastically cooks and eats it with great gusto and frequency. And we do eat a lot of monkfish in Ireland—it's a succulent and meaty fish I think is greatly undervalued in the US. This is a wonderful way to get to know it and to show it off. You can make it with other fish, and you can leave out the beans or add more of them. I've even left out the fish and made it vegetarian for some Hindu friends visiting Ireland, and they smacked their lips over every bite. The decidedly French addition of pastis underlines the anise flavor of the fennel, another vegetable we eat a lot of in Ireland. The French would probably just eat this in a dish, maybe with some crusty bread, but my dad always served it in deep soup plates on top of a mound of extra-creamy mashed potatoes.

*Makes 6 servings*

3 tablespoons olive oil
1 large yellow onion, diced
3 garlic cloves, minced
2 fennel bulbs, trimmed and cut into wedges
2 16-ounce cans whole peeled tomatoes, with their juices
1 cup dry white wine
2 sprigs rosemary
3 tablespoons pastis
1 15-ounce can cooked white beans, drained and rinsed
1 ½ pounds monkfish fillets, cut into 2-inch pieces
¼ cup crème fraiche (or heavy cream)
Salt and pepper

1   Heat the olive oil in a large, heavy stewpot over medium heat and add the onions and garlic. Cook, stirring until the onions are softened but not browned, 4 to 5 minutes. Add the fennel and cook for 2 to 3 minutes more, until slightly softened.

2   Add the tomatoes and their juices, breaking the tomatoes up against the sides of the pan. Add the wine and rosemary, and bring the stew to a boil. Reduce heat, cover, and simmer for about 20 minutes, until the fennel is tender.

3   Add the pastis and white beans, and heat through. With the stew bubbling, gently lay the monkfish in the pot, pushing it into the mixture so it's coated in the hot liquid. Cover the pan and cook for another 5 to 7 minutes, until the fish is opaque.

4   Stir in the crème fraiche or cream to lighten the mixture to a pale orange. Season with salt and pepper. Serve soon, so your fish doesn't get tough sitting in the hot liquid.

# IRISH SEAFOOD CHOWDER

We're not interested in the authentically thin chowders of New England's heritage. At any pub in Ireland worth its lunchtime credentials, you can get a bowl of thick and decadently creamy chowder, and the best ones are loaded with a range of seafood. Mussels are always present, and usually chunks of whitefish and perhaps some salmon, and sometimes a few shrimp and maybe clams. It's a glorious meal, made all the better with the usual accompaniment of brown bread and butter. The creamy, buttery taste that underpins the flavor of the fresh seafood? That's cream. And butter.

*Makes 6 to 8 servings*

½ cup (1 stick) butter

1 large leek, white and part of the green, very thinly sliced and washed

1 medium yellow onion, diced small

1 small carrot, peeled and grated

⅓ cup all-purpose flour

2 cups bottled clam juice

4 cups whole milk

1 cup dry white wine

1 cup light cream

8 ounces fish (such as salmon or whitefish or a mix of the two), cut in 1-inch pieces

8 ounces cooked mussels, without shells

8 ounces small cooked clams, without shells

4 ounces small shrimp, without shells (cooked or raw)

Salt and pepper

1 In a large stew or soup pot over medium heat, melt the butter and stir in the leeks, onion, and grated carrot. Cover the pan and cook the vegetables until completely softened but not at all browned, about 10 to 12 minutes, stirring once or twice.

2 Sprinkle the flour over the vegetables and stir to combine. Slowly stir in the clam juice or fish stock, adding it gradually to avoid lumps. Blend in the milk, wine, and cream, stirring continually to avoid lumps. Bring to a simmer and cook, stirring frequently for 10 to 15 minutes, until the soup is thickened and the vegetables are tender.

3 Add the seafood and heat through to cook any pieces that need it. Serve hot, with a sprinkle of parsley.

# FISH AND SEAFOOD

## 4

## To Force Oysters

Take half a quart good oysters without their beards, 5 large anchovies pound them together, put to them some chives thyme a good deal of parsley cut very small a lump of butter some crumbs of bread as for scallops put them in your shells and brown them.

—from an 18<sup>th</sup> century Irish cookbook manuscript

For an island-dwelling nation, over the centuries, the Irish didn't really embrace fish the way you might imagine. I think in many ways, it was just too much of a good thing. Fish and seafood were everywhere, fast and cheap, so it was food for poor people, and in fact servants' agreements from the nineteenth century sometimes included clauses that they didn't have to eat salmon more than a certain number of times per week. (Rich people ate beef, which isn't that surprising when you consider cows were used as a measure of wealth in ancient Ireland.) It took awhile for us to realize our salmon was (and admittedly, I'm biased) the best in the entire world. It's so rich and flavorful, moist and curdy—today when I'm home, I gorge myself on salmon, fresh and smoked; when I'm in New York, I spurn lox, because it's got nothing—and I mean nothing—on Irish smoked salmon, which has a freshness, delicacy, and distinct lack of oiliness that puts other smoked fish to shame.

Nowadays, after the western world's food revolution, we've finally grasped that our fish is something special, so I suppose it makes sense that the finest preparations are the simplest.

# WHOLE BAKED SALMON

Suppose you come into possession of a whole salmon. There's not much to do besides cook it whole. Filleting it yourself is a thankless job, and it's not necessary. Cooked, the flesh flakes off in beautiful chunks. Considering how rich and fatty salmon is, it's kind of interesting that the sauce that compliments it best is mayonnaise. Together, the two fats meld into a lushness and richness that makes you reach for just one more forkful. Either make a homemade mayonnaise from a recipe you like, or doctor a good-quality mayo with a little extra lemon juice, and serve a bowlful on the side to dollop next to each serving of salmon. If you want the classic over-the-top presentation, seen at parties and buffets, take the skin off the finished salmon, leaving the head intact, and slather the body lavishly with mayo. Then cut thin slices of cucumber and layer them all over the fish like scales.

GO WILD
Farmed salmon is available in Ireland, but aficionados prefer wild salmon. (True aficionados like to catch their wild salmon themselves!) Wild salmon has very pale pink flesh and a more delicate flavor than farmed. Wild salmon is increasingly available again in the US, and it's worth seeking out the best, freshest wild salmon you can find to make this recipe. Find out when your fish seller gets the delivery and buy then.

Makes 8 to 10 servings
Butter
1 whole salmon, 5 to 6 pounds, cleaned and scaled,
   head and tail intact
Salt and pepper
1 lemon, sliced
Small bunch fresh parsley

1   Preheat the oven to 350 degrees F. Tear off a large sheet of aluminum foil, large enough to wrap the fish, and lay it on a baking sheet. Butter the center of the foil where the fish will be. Lay the fish on the foil and salt and pepper the interior cavity. Stuff the parsley into the cavity and lay the lemon slices on top of the parsley. Dot the exterior with butter along the body and sprinkle with salt and pepper.

2   Tent the foil over the salmon, loosely sealing the top without touching the skin. Bake for 1 ½ hours, until the flesh flakes easily with a fork. Serve warm, at room temperature, or chilled.

# FISH CAKES

When I was a kid, I loved it when we had fish cakes, and I'm glad to say I have a fish-loving son who feels the same. His eyes light up and he says things like, "Wow, fish cakes?! Hooray! Can I help mix them?" (To keep it in perspective, my other son says things like, "Not for me. Can't I have peanut butter instead?") And despite the fact that fish cakes are an excellent way to use up leftover fish and leftover mashed potatoes (as is Family Fish Pie, p. 90), Fish Cakes are still a treat. I like them with a squeeze of lemon and some tartar sauce.

*Makes 6 servings*

3 cups flaked cooked whitefish
    fillets or salmon
2 cups leftover mashed potatoes
2 hard-boiled eggs, mashed with a
    fork
¼ cup chopped fresh parsley
Salt and pepper
1 egg, beaten
¼ cup all-purpose flour
Oil for frying

1   Combine the fish, potatoes, hardboiled eggs, and parsley gently, trying not to break up the fish too much. Taste and add salt and pepper if needed. When the seasoning is correct, gently mix in the beaten egg to bind the mixture.

2   Form into 12 fat little cakes, about 1 inch thick, and set them on a plate. If you want to do this early in the day, cover them with plastic wrap and chill them until you're ready to cook.

3   When ready to cook them, preheat the oven to 180 degrees F and put the flour on a plate. Stir in ½ teaspoon salt and ¼ teaspoon pepper. Heat about ¼ inch of oil in a large skillet over medium heat. Working in batches, roll the cakes in the seasoned flour and fry in the hot oil, turning once, until golden, about 4 minutes per side. (You may need a little more time if the cakes were refrigerated.)

4   Put the finished cakes on a heatproof platter, and keep them warm in the oven while you finish frying the rest. Don't crowd the pan, or you won't have room for flipping without breaking them.

# FAMILY FISH PIE

In my experience, there is no fish pie in America when it comes to standard family suppers. Meatloaf, spaghetti, chili—those are the sort of fallbacks that occupy the same place in the American kitchen that fish pie, or Shepherd's Pie (p. 128), or Cottage Pie (p. 128), occupies in the Irish kitchen. This is a good basic version, but you can use any leftover fish and combination of vegetables you have. My brother Andrew, who's a chef, always uses chopped fennel instead of celery. He's also the one who advised me to use an equal amount of smoked whitefish with the whitefish for the best flavor (it is good) and to go sparingly on the salmon (avoid smoked salmon) because too much imparts an oily flavor to the pie. A little salmon enriches it—as does the cream.

*Makes 6 servings*

2 tablespoons butter

1 tablespoon olive oil

2 leeks, white and green parts, thinly sliced and washed

2 sticks celery, roughly chopped

1 large carrot, peeled and shredded

2 tablespoons all-purpose flour

2 teaspoons mustard (either Dijon or a hot English mustard such as Colman's)

2 cups whole milk or light cream, plus 2 to 3 tablespoons more if needed

¼ teaspoon ground nutmeg

1 sprig rosemary

1 bay leaf

1 pound boneless whitefish fillets (cod, monkfish, turbot, whiting, pollock), cut in small chunks

1 pound smoked fish (smoked trout, smoked haddock), cut in small chunks

8 ounces boneless, skinless salmon, cut into small chunks

½ teaspoon salt (less, or none, if your smoked fish is salty—taste a bit and see)

½ teaspoon black pepper

6 cups mashed potatoes

½ cup shredded cheddar or parmesan

1   Preheat the oven to 350 degrees F and butter a 3 or 4-quart baking dish (you can use a 9 x 13-inch dish but a deeper pan is preferable).

2   Put the oil and butter in a skillet over medium heat. Stir in the leeks, celery, and carrots and cover. Cook for 10 to 12 minutes, until the vegetables are completely tender but not browned.

3   Stir in the flour and mustard, then gradually add in the milk or light cream, stirring constantly to avoid lumps. Add the salt, pepper, nutmeg, rosemary, and bay leaf, and cook for 2 to 3 minutes until the sauce is simmering.

4   Add all the fish pieces, stirring gently to avoid breaking them up too much. Turn this mixture into the prepared dish. Stir the mashed potatoes, adding a bit of milk if necessary to loosen them, and spoon them in an even layer over the fish. Use the tines of a fork to make craggy peaks in the potatoes; this helps make a nicely browned crust later. Top with the cheese and bake for 50 to 60 minutes, until bubbly golden brown on top.

# CHEESY BAKED FISH

Irish cheese used to be all but nonexistent, but in recent years a new crop of artisan cheese makers has been taking advantage of all the excellent dairy in Ireland to produce some excellent Irish-made cheeses. A cook (not to mention an eater) is spoiled for choice, especially at a cheesemonger such as Sheridans in Dublin, where the finest cheeses lie, aged to perfection, and just begging you to take them home. You can use any hard cheese for this recipe, but avoid fatty, softer cheeses like Havarti or Fontina. Melted, they're too greasy to work well.

The Italians will tell you cheese and fish never go together. The Irish disagree mightily. The beauty of this is its utter ease—and how well it turns out every time. Use any meaty whitefish that looks good in the market. Haddock is ideal, and I like cod here too.

Make 6 servings

2½ pounds meaty whitefish, such as haddock or cod
Salt and pepper
2 tablespoons mustard, such as Dijon or spicy brown
   (or 1 tablespoon sharp English mustard such as Colman's)
2 cups shredded hard cheese, such as cheddar or gruyere
½ cup heavy cream
¾ cup soft breadcrumbs (from 2 slices of bread)
¼ cup chopped fresh parsley

1   Preheat the oven to 375 degrees F and lightly grease a shallow baking dish.

2   Lay the fish fillets in the dish in a single layer or only slightly overlapping, and sprinkle them lightly with salt and pepper. Spread the mustard over the fillets, cover with the cheese, and drizzle with the cream. Scatter the breadcrumbs and parsley over all.

3   Bake for 25 to 30 minutes, until the fish is opaque and the topping is golden brown.

Cheeses at the English Market, Cork

# DUBLIN LAWYER

Any Irish cookbook has to contain this traditional recipe, even if we don't eat it all the time, because the mockery of it so appeals to the Irish the dish lives on and on. Perhaps it's apocryphal that the name came about because this expensive dish so full of luxury is best suited to, or perhaps only afforded by, those who practice law for a living—in fact, I'm usually suspicious of culinary history that is so pat—but by now it's an accepted tale and the grim humor of it appeals particularly to post-boom Ireland.

Once you get past that part of the story, it's an excellent way to loll in the decadence of a good, large crustacean—don't bother with anything less than the outrageous expense of a two-pound lobster. Considering the whole thing could have easily been prepared over a silver chafing dish, it's easy to conjure up the scene Thackeray described when he ate Dublin Lawyer on a trip to Ireland in 1847, of pink-cheeked legal gentlemen, merry and bewigged, preparing this in their chambers after a day in court. If you have a chafing dish or hotplate, Dublin Lawyer still makes for excellent tableside drama today. Don't be frightened by the huge whoosh of flame that comes from setting the hot whiskey alight in the pan; it will burn off in seconds, and you can always clap down a lid if you're worried. Just keep your face out of the way.

For 2 servings, easily doubled

1 large lobster, about 2 pounds, freshly boiled or steamed
½ cup (1 stick) butter
½ cup Irish whiskey
½ cup heavy cream
Salt and pepper

1   Crack and shell the lobster, removing the meat in large chunks. Depending on the size of the tail, tear or cut it into two or four pieces for easy serving.

2   In a chafing dish or large skillet over a medium heat, melt the butter. As it begins to sizzle (and not a moment later), add the lobster meat to the pan and toss to coat well and heat through, 1 to 2 minutes.

3   Pour in the whiskey. After a moment, when it has heated through (cold whiskey won't flame), touch a lighted match to the edge of the pan, or, if you're cooking over flame, tilt the pan so the whiskey's fumes can come into contact with the light under the pan. The alcohol will burn with a rush, throwing up an exciting and dramatic flame that will burn right off, removing the raw taste of the whiskey and leaving mellow smokiness behind.

4   Pour in the cream and let it bubble. Season liberally with salt and pepper and eat immediately.

# HOWTH SCALLOPS WITH BEURRE BLANC

Supposing you have a dozen plump, succulent scallops from Dublin Bay, perhaps with the coral still attached, this is the only way to serve them. Irish scallops (and again, I'm deeply biased) are the absolute best I have ever eaten: Fat and flavorful, they are nearly as big as the palm of my hand, and they always have the coral attached. The coral, if you've not heard of it, is an orange-red comma of custardy flavor that is best described as analogous to a lobster's tomalley. Most Irish seafood is in stores the day it's caught, so the bright pink-orange coral attached is a great indicator of freshness, because it gets discolored very quickly.

In high-quality American fish stores, you may be able to order scallops with the coral attached. Otherwise, look for the plumpest diver scallops you can find. They should be beautifully moist, not at all wet, which is an indication they've been soaked in a brine or perhaps (ugh) a preservative. If in doubt, ask.

What about that Beurre Blanc? Kind of French, right? Well, my dad always served them this way, and it's exquisite, but to be adamantly Irish, just cook them in a large amount of foaming butter until the edges brown and the scallop is white through (do *not* overcook!), and serve with a generous squeeze of lemon.

Serves 6 as an appetizer or 2 to 3 as a main course

For the beurre blanc:

¼ cup dry white wine

2 tablespoons white wine vinegar

1 small shallot, very finely chopped

2 tablespoons heavy cream

¾ cups (1½ sticks) butter

1 lemon

Salt and pepper

For the scallops:

12 large scallops

Salt and pepper

2 to 3 tablespoons butter

1  For perfection, turn the oven to 180 degrees F and heat the
   serving plates and a platter while you make the beurre blanc: In a
   medium-sized heavy saucepan over medium heat, pour the wine
   and vinegar, and add the shallots. Bring to a boil, reduce heat,
   and simmer very gently for 5 to 6 minutes, to reduce the liquid by
   about 2/3, and cook the shallots to just tender.

2  Pour in the cream and cook to heat through and thicken slightly.
   Cut the butter into 8 pieces and drop them in one at a time,
   whisking well after each addition to fully incorporate the butter
   into the sauce. When all the butter is added, season with freshly
   squeezed lemon juice, salt, and pepper. You can do this to taste,
   adding more or less of all three as you like. (A French chef would
   strain out the shallots now, but I never do.) Set the beurre blanc
   aside on the back of the stove to keep warm.

3  Season the scallops on both sides with a little salt and pepper. Put
   a tablespoon or two of butter in a skillet over medium-high heat.
   As soon as it sizzles, shake the pan to distribute it evenly and lay
   in half the scallops, being sure not to overcrowd. Cook for about
   4 minutes, until golden on the edge, and then flip, cooking for 3
   to 4 minutes until the other side is golden. The flesh should be
   just white throughout. Remove to the warm platter and cook the
   remaining scallops the same way.

4  To serve, divide the beurre blanc in pools among the warm plates,
   reserving a little for the top. Lift the scallops onto the plates and
   drizzle the rest on top. Serve immediately.

# STUFFED MUSSELS

When I went to art college in the west of Ireland, in County Sligo, there were often times when I had too much month left at the end of my money. Because I lived in a cottage on the coast, fortunately I was able to forage for a fair amount of food. There was "sea spinach," a seaweed that was like nettles when cooked, blackberries, and nettles in season. I was able to catch the occasional rabbit or pheasant, too. But the most reliable source of food was the mussels that clung to the rocks in huge colonies near the old boathouse down by the shore. I gathered them in large quantities, soaked them overnight in fresh water with a little flour in it to disgorge them, then scrubbed off their "beards" and cooked them in many and various ways. This is one of my favorites, sort of like a mussel version of "Clams Casino," and it's a standard on Irish menus. In Ireland, you can even buy them already prepped in packages at the grocery store, ready to be popped under a broiler. Serve with fresh lemon wedges, if you like, to squeeze over each as you eat it.

Makes 8 appetizer servings or 4 main course servings

**3 pounds fresh, live mussels, shells shut tight**

**2 cups soft fresh bread crumbs**
**¼ cup softened butter (or olive oil)**
**¼ cup grated Parmesan**
**3 garlic cloves, minced**
**½ cup chopped parsley**
**Salt and pepper**

1 Preheat oven to 450 degrees F. Scrub the mussels well and be sure they're all tight shut, or will shut tight if you tap them.

2 Put them in a large soup pot and add about 2 inches of water. Bring it to a boil over high heat, cover and boil for 3 to 4 minutes, until the mussels open.

3 Drain and cool, discarding any unopened mussels. Pull off and discard the upper shell and arrange the mussels on the half shell on a large rimmed baking sheet.

4 Stir together the remaining ingredients, and top each mussel with a spoonful of this mixture. Bake for 5 to 7 minutes, until the topping is bubbly and crisp. Eat hot.

# Oysters and Guinness

By now, you may be starting to note the recurrent theme of brown bread and butter as an accompaniment to all sorts of Irish dishes. But nowhere is the trinity so sacred as buttered brown bread with oysters and Guinness. It's the quintessential taste of Ireland in one bite. Assuming you're in Ireland, it's simple to perform the rite:

1   Raise aloft a fresh oyster in its half-shell—with or without a squeeze of lemon, your call—and tip it with all the juices into your eager mouth.

2   Take a bite of buttered brown bread and give the whole thing a couple quick chews.

3   Wash it all down with a slug of creamy and cool Guinness.

Reflect on the pure pleasure, and repeat until you're done. At an event such as the Galway Oyster Festival, you might not be done until the end of the day or into the night.

# DUBLIN BAY SCAMPI

They're *like* langoustine, and my wife from the American South thought they were crawfish the first time she saw them, but Dublin Bay prawns are a distinct breed, kind of like a cross between a large shrimp and a small, succulent lobster. It's almost a joke that one of our favorite things to do with them is bread and deep-fry them to be eaten with chips, a deluxe pub snack that's near-impossible to replicate anywhere else. If you come into possession of a batch of Dublin Bay prawns, your other option is simply to sauté them in butter with some garlic, salt, and pepper, but not only is deep-frying more common, it's really, really good. Serve the fried prawns with tartar sauce or tangy pink Marie Rose sauce, p. 308—or both.

Makes 2 to 3 servings

**Oil for deep-frying**
**½ cup all-purpose flour**
**1 teaspoon salt**
**½ teaspoon black pepper**
**2 eggs**
**2 cups breadcrumbs**
**1 pound Dublin Bay prawns (or langoustines, or large shrimp in a pinch), shelled**

1  Put the oil in a large, heavy saucepan, and heat it over medium heat to 365 degrees F (a deep-frying thermometer is indispensable).

2  Put the flour in a bowl and toss it with the salt and pepper. Break the eggs into a bowl and beat them lightly with a fork. Put the breadcrumbs in a bowl. Pat the prawns dry with a paper towel.

3  When the oil is ready, dip each prawn in the flour, then the egg, then the breadcrumbs, turning it in each to coat, and drop it carefully into the hot oil. Work in small batches. Fry them for 5 to 6 minutes, until each one is golden. Use a slotted spoon to lift them onto a paper towel–lined plate. Repeat with remaining prawns. Eat hot.

# FISH AND CHIPS

The ingredients are basic, so freshness counts. Use good potatoes and very fresh fish; a white one such as cod, flounder, sole, whiting, or halibut is best. Although floury russets are more like typical Irish potatoes, yellow-fleshed potatoes such as Yukon Gold make excellent chips, too. Real lard (not the super-processed, supermarket stuff) does impart a flavor and a perfect finish, but corn, canola, or peanut oil are perhaps more practical as well as good for frying at high temperatures.

*Makes 4 hefty servings*

**4 pounds potatoes**
**1½ cups flour**
**1 teaspoon baking soda**
**½ teaspoon salt**
**1 cup water**
**2 quarts of oil for deep-frying**
**1½ pounds white fish fillets**

1 Peel the potatoes and cut them into thick fries. Have a large bowl of cold water nearby, and toss the cut fries into it as you work. Set aside while you make the batter.

2 Combine the flour, baking soda, and salt in a medium bowl, then slowly whisk in water until a smooth paste is formed. Add a little more water if the batter doesn't lie flat in the bowl—it shouldn't be thick or fluffy. Cover and set aside to rest for 30 minutes.

3 While the batter rests, heat 2 quarts of oil to 330 degrees F in a large, deep, heavy-bottomed pan with tall sides.

(If you don't have a thermometer, throw in a cube of bread or a fry. If it sizzles, it's ready, but using a thermometer is best.) Remove the potatoes from the water and dry them well with a clean, absorbent kitchen towel or two.

4 Cook the chips in three or four batches for the first frying. (The second frying can be more crowded.) Carefully put the first batch into the 330 degrees F oil, avoiding crowding, and fry for 5 minutes or until they start to brown, stirring a couple of times to avoid their sticking together. Remove from oil and place them in big bowl well-lined with absorbent paper towels. They should be cooked through and soft, but they'll look soggy and undercooked.

5 Cut fish filets into 6-inch lengths. (Leave whole if fillets are small.) Make sure oil heat has returned to 350 degrees F. Dip each fillet into batter and slip gently into hot oil. Fry until golden brown, approximately 5 minutes. When the fish is done, drain on a paper towel.

6 Raise the oil heat to 375 degrees F to do the second frying. Put the chips back in, in slightly larger batches, until they are crisp and golden, 1 to 2 minutes. Remove from the oil and drain on fresh paper towels, then season with salt.

7 Serve hot fish and chips immediately, with tartar sauce and ketchup or with salt and malt vinegar (not any other kind of vinegar).

Fay's Butcher Shop, Thomas St. Dublin

# MEAT AND GAME

## 5

## To Pickle Beef Pork, etc.

Cut your beef or pork into what size you please put into salt and water for twenty four hours then take it out and drain and wipe it, make a pickle strong enough to bear one egg of soft water, bay salt, common salt and salt petre and brown sugar boil and scum it and when it is cold pour it on your meat which must not be packed too close, this does ham or tongues.

—from an 18th century Irish cookbook manuscript

An Irish butcher shop is a glorious place—there's a huge turnover, as you might imagine in such a land of carnivores—and in country butcher shops, the proprietor very often is raising his own animals and overseeing their slaughter. It's hard to get much more local than that, and it shows in the quality of the products. In Dublin, Cork, and larger towns, the bigger butcher shops frequently make their own sausages and cure their own rashers and bacon.

Every year at Christmas, even after my parents had moved back to Dublin from the County Meath town where I grew up, we still made the pilgrimage out to Tony Darby's, my dad's favorite butcher, to collect a veritable locker full of meat: The turkey (or sometimes a goose), always with the head and feet still attached to assess the quality; its twin for the Christmas table, an enormous ham; the raft of thick-cut steaks, from prime grass-fed (always) cattle; the dense and weighty spiced beef, to have for cutting sandwiches or impromptu meals; and the endless rashers, sausages, and puddings we'd require for leisurely holiday breakfasts. Once we'd laid in enough meat for any eventuality over the next couple weeks, the holidays could commence.

# STUFFED PORK CHOPS

"Double-cut" chops are often seen in Irish butcher shops, and the term means they're twice the thickness of regular chops. They're intended to be stuffed with a light stuffing, not a heavy, wet one, usually a herby one made of breadcrumbs, onion, and celery. I particularly like mine with a little apple and sage. This same stuffing can be used for poultry, and if you like your stuffing a little more damp, wet it with up to a cup of chicken stock. For the chops, though, make it as below—they get too weighed down with a wet stuffing.

Makes 6 servings

For the stuffing:

¼ cup (½ stick) butter

1 small yellow onion, diced

1 celery stalk, thinly sliced

1 large tart apple, peeled, cored, and diced small

¼ cup chopped fresh parsley

2 teaspoons fresh sage leaves, thinly sliced

1 teaspoon fresh thyme leaves, chopped

2 cups soft breadcrumbs

Salt and pepper

6 double-cut boneless pork loin chops (about 1½ inches thick)

2 tablespoons vegetable oil

1   Preheat the oven to 350 degrees F and lightly grease a 9 × 13-inch baking dish.

2   In a large skillet over medium heat, melt the butter and stir in the onion and celery. Cook for 5 to 6 minutes until softened and translucent. Add the apple and continue to cook for 3 to 4 minutes to soften the apple slightly. Stir in the parsley and sage. Add the breadcrumbs and toss to combine. Sprinkle with salt and pepper and spoon the stuffing into a bowl to cool slightly.

3   Wipe out the skillet with a paper towel. With a sharp paring knife, cut a large pocket inside each chop, working the knife parallel to the surface and making an opening about 2 inches wide at the side of each chop, opening the pocket wider inside the chop. With a spoon, fill each chop with about a ½ cup of stuffing, pressing and packing it in.

4   Put the wiped skillet over medium-high heat and add a tablespoon of the cooking oil. When the oil shimmers over the heat, put in the first three chops and brown the first side well, 5 to 6 minutes. Flip and brown the other side for another 3 to 4 minutes. Lay the first three chops in the prepared baking dish and repeat with the remaining three.

5   Cover the dish with aluminum foil and bake for about 45 minutes, until an instant-read thermometer in the center of the stuffing reads 150 degrees F.

## STUFFED PORK TENDERLOIN

The same apple and herb stuffing in the pork chops makes an excellent filling for pork tenderloin. Pick up a 3-pound, boneless center-cut pork loin and ask the butcher or meat department at your supermarket to butterfly it. Preheat the oven to 350 degrees F and prepare the stuffing as directed. Sprinkle the meat with salt and pepper and spread the stuffing over opened butterflied loin. Roll it up tightly, securing it with butcher's string by tying knots every 1 ½ to 2 inches. As with the chops, brown the rolled loin on all sides. Place in a baking dish and roast for 50 to 60 minutes until a thermometer stuck in the center of the roast registers 150 degrees F. Let rest 10 to 15 minutes before slicing.

# ROAST PORK WITH CRACKLING

Americans are missing so much when it comes to roast pork, because roasts in the States are almost always sold with the skin trimmed off. They usually have a layer of fat, which is great for flavor, but it's the unattractive skin outside the fat, like a thick rind, that roasts up into crisp crackling, sort of like those bags of fried pork rinds but infinitely better. Once in a while, I actually do see skin on a roast at the supermarket, and these days in my neighborhood I know a butcher whom I can ask when I want crackling. Try to do the same. You'll be glad. To make proper crackling, you have to score the skin before you cook. In Ireland, the butcher does this for you. An American butcher may do so as well. The skin is really hard to cut so I find when I do the job at home that a box-cutter style knife works best.

Makes 6 to 8 servings

**5-pound loin of pork with the skin still on**
**Salt and pepper**

1  Preheat the oven to 375 degrees F. Using a craft knife or Stanley knife, score the skin at ½-inch intervals. Rub salt liberally all over the skin, working it into the slits with your hands. Sprinkle well with pepper.

2  Roast for 90 minutes. After the first 40 minutes, baste with the pan juices every 20 minutes or so, if you think of it. (While I do think basting helps, I've made other roasts where I totally forgot to baste, and it was still excellent.)

3  After 90 minutes, take the roast out of the oven and turn up the heat to 475 degrees F. Remove the roast from the roasting pan and put it on a rimmed baking sheet. Return it to the oven for 10 to 15 minutes. This will get the crackling really crisp and crunchy right at the end. If it's not super-crisp, it's hard and chewy and not nearly as appealing. And you have to switch to a new baking sheet so you don't burn all the pan juices onto the roasting pan you were using.

4  Let the roast rest for 10 minutes before slicing.

# ROAST LEG OF LAMB

Lamb in Ireland is a given. We eat it all the time, and sheep are everywhere when you're driving through the countryside. At the butcher shop, lamb and pork definitely predominate, letting beef lag behind in a distinct third place. I think it's because our lamb is so good, with a much more delicate flavor than you may expect if your primary experience with it is a roast leg of American lamb duly cooked in the spring and eaten with mint jelly. And here's something important: We do not eat mint jelly in Ireland. We eat our lamb in the spring with a tangy, savory mint sauce of fresh mint and vinegar (see p. 308). Another key thing: Lamb should be well-done, nearly crisped on the outside but decidedly pink and very juicy on the inside. Overcooked lamb is gray and dry and simply won't taste good.

*Makes 8 servings*

**1 (7- to 8-pound) leg of lamb, bone in**
**4 cloves garlic, cut into slivers**
**½ cup (1 stick) butter, softened**
**1 tablespoon salt**
**1 teaspoon black pepper**
**2 tablespoons fresh rosemary leaves, chopped**
**Mint Sauce, (p. 308)**

1   Preheat oven to 450 degrees F. With a sharp knife, cut small slits about 2 inches deep all over the leg of lamb. Poke a sliver of garlic into each slit.

2   In small bowl, cream the softened butter with the salt, pepper, and rosemary. Put lamb in a shallow roasting pan, and smear the mixture generously over the lamb.

3   Roast for about 25 minutes to sear the meat, then lower heat to 350 degrees F and roast for about 1 hour, until the internal temperature is approximately 170 degrees F. Do not overcook.

4   Let the lamb rest for 10 minutes before slicing thin. Spoon pools of mint sauce onto plates next to sliced lamb for dipping.

# STUFFED LEG OF LAMB

Since we eat so much lamb, eating it roasted with mint sauce can get old fast. Whereas a butterflied leg of lamb can be stuffed with all sorts of good things, rolled and roasted, keeping it perpetually interesting. The garlicky, herby mixture here, supplemented with a handful of golden raisins to play off the meat's natural sweetness, was a particular favorite of my father, but it's also very good with the bread and apple mixture used to stuff the pork chops on p. 108.

*Makes 6 to 8 servings*

1 boneless leg of lamb, 4 to 5 pounds, butterflied
Salt and pepper
½ cup golden raisins
4 to 6 garlic cloves, minced
¼ cup fresh rosemary leaves, chopped
1 tablespoon fresh thyme leaves
Zest and juice of 1 lemon
Extra virgin olive oil

1   Preheat the oven to 350 degrees F and fit a roasting rack into a roasting pan.

2   Open out the butterflied lamb, with the meaty side upward. Season it liberally with salt and pepper. Scatter the raisins, garlic, rosemary, thyme, and the lemon zest across the top, and squeeze the lemon juice over all. Drizzle with olive oil and roll the lamb up firmly, starting with the long side. Use butcher's string to tie it off every 1 ½ inches.

3   Drizzle more olive oil into a large skillet over medium-high heat. Sprinkle the outside of the roast liberally with salt and pepper. Put the roast into the skillet and sear it on all sides to brown.

4   Transfer the seared, rolled lamb to the roasting rack in the pan and roast in the oven for 60 to 70 minutes, until an instant-read thermometer inserted in the center reads 140 degrees F for rare or 150 degrees F for medium. If you cook it past medium, you'll have tough, gray, nearly inedible meat, and you'll be very sorry.

# HOLIDAY SPICED BEEF

The day after Christmas in Ireland is known as St. Stephen's Day, and the done thing is to go out on a walk or a hike and try to make up for our overindulgences of the day before. My family used to go beagling, which is like hunting, except we walked after a pack of dogs instead of riding horses, and the dogs weren't actually chasing anything but a dragged scent. It's like Hunting Lite, but we sure worked up a fierce appetite that was then quenched by standing over the boot of the car, passing around some flasks of hot tea and others of whiskey, and eating spiced beef sandwiches. Spiced beef is a little like pastrami, but sweeter and spicier, and it wouldn't be Christmas in Ireland without it. Many people buy theirs from a butcher, but it's not too hard to make at home. Saltpeter is a preservative you can buy at the pharmacy in Ireland, and it helps give the beef its color. If you prefer, leave it out.

Makes 12 to 15 servings

5-pound rump of beef
¼ cup dark brown sugar
2 tablespoons ground allspice
2 teaspoons saltpeter
½ cup coarse kosher salt

1   On the first day: Rub the beef all over with brown sugar and place it in a glass or ceramic dish. Cover with plastic wrap and refrigerate overnight.

2   On the second day: Combine the allspice and saltpeter and rub them on the sugar-coated beef. Cover with plastic wrap and refrigerate overnight.

3   On the third day: Rub the beef with salt. Cover with plastic wrap and refrigerate for 7 days.

4   On the tenth day: put the beef in a large soup pot and cover with water. Bring to a boil and simmer gently for two hours.

5   Put it in a casserole dish and cover the casserole loosely with a large sheet of plastic wrap that overhangs the edges rather than seals the top tightly. Lay a plate that's smaller than the casserole upside down on top of the covered beef and weight the plate down with a couple heavy cans so that it really pushes down on the meat. Refrigerate for 48 hours. This compresses the meat and makes the final product more pastrami-like. Serve cold, sliced thin.

# SAUSAGES IN PUFF PASTRY

As I've said elsewhere, we eat sausages all the time in Ireland—for breakfast, for birthday parties, for finger food at any gathering. But for special occasions, we like to wrap our sausages in pastry. It's like donning a suit for a party.

*Makes about 2 dozen, depending on sausage size*
**All-purpose flour**
**1 pound frozen puff pastry, thawed**
**1 pound Irish sausages (p. 34)**
**1 egg**

1   Preheat the oven to 425 degrees F and lightly grease two baking sheets. Scatter flour on a clean work surface and roll out one sheet of the thawed pastry to flatten it slightly. Lay down a raw sausage on one edge of the pastry, parallel to the side, and fold the shorter end of the pastry over it to wrap it. Unwrap and cut out that rectangle of pastry. So, assuming you have a 4-inch sausage, a 4- or 5-inch square of pastry is all you need to cover it. (It's okay to leave the ends uncovered, but it's also okay to wrap them.)

2   Cut the pastry and wrap all the sausages. Use a fork to press the edges down to make a tight seal. (If they're not sealing firmly, you may need to brush a little water along the edge of the pastry before closing them over.) Lay them on the baking sheet with 2 inches in between each sausage roll.

3   When all the sausages and pastry are used (you can reroll pastry as needed, but it will get a little flattened), use a sharp knife to make several long slits on top of each roll. Beat the egg with 2 tablespoons water in a small bowl, and brush it over the surface of each sausage roll.

4   Bake until the pastry is golden and the sausages are cooked through, about 20 minutes. Serve hot or at room temperature. You can also make these the day before and reheat them for 10 minutes at 350 degrees F.

# GRILLED LAMB CHOPS

Simple is best when it comes to high-quality lamb chops, but I still can't help gilding the lily a bit with some garlic, fresh herbs, and good olive oil. Lamb takes so well to garlic and rosemary you might think we've got some Italian in us in Ireland, but rosemary, in fact, grows beautifully there and we use it frequently. Despite how far north Ireland is—on the map, we're on a par with Newfoundland—our climate remains mostly mild and temperate because we're washed by the Gulf Stream, and rosemary bushes thrive. After parsley and thyme, it's the most common herb in our kitchens.

Makes 6 servings
6 lamb loin chops, about 1½ inches thick
Salt and pepper
2 garlic cloves, minced
1 tablespoon fresh rosemary leaves
Extra-virgin olive oil

1   Lay the lamb chops in a dish and sprinkle with salt and pepper. Scatter on the garlic and rosemary and drizzle with olive oil, rubbing the aromatics in with your fingers. Leave to marinate for at least 30 minutes, or as long as overnight.

2   To cook, preheat a broiler on high. Broil the chops 6 inches from the broiler for 10 minutes per side until browned and sizzling but still medium-rare inside. If you don't have a powerful broiler, preheat the oven to 425 degrees F. Heat a cast-iron skillet over medium-high heat and drizzle with olive oil. Brown the chops on each side for 1 to 2 minutes, and then put the skillet in the oven. Cook for 10 minutes, until medium-rare. Let the lamb chops rest for 5 minutes before serving.

# IRISH BOILED BACON AND CABBAGE

This is the thing we're eating when you think we're eating corned beef—which we're not, or mostly not. As I've mentioned before, there *are* small pockets of corned beef–eaters in Ireland, mostly in Cork and around Munster, but it's very uncommon, and I went my whole life without ever tasting it until I came to America. Those who do eat corned beef in Ireland swear by it, however; I once told a reporter at a regional American newspaper we don't eat corned beef in Ireland, and when she mentioned that as part of a St. Patrick's Day food story, she got an extremely irate letter from a expat Corkwoman who said the reporter and I had offended the memory of her dead mother!

So while I'm batting a thousand, I may as well offend someone else's Irish granny by pointing out we do *not* boil and eat those heavy, hard heads of greeny-white cabbage you see in so many corned beef suppers in America. We make coleslaw out of those, same as Americans. The cabbage we boil is called spring cabbage, or York cabbage, and it's a big, loose bunch of deep, dark greens, full of flavor and texture, and it doesn't become waterlogged. The best substitute I can recommend is savoy cabbage. Some people like to boil the cabbage with the bacon at the end of cooking time, but at my house, we always cooked the cabbage separately.

The typical accompaniment is boiled potatoes. I'm partial to a bit of mustard with my bacon, but some people prefer Parsley Sauce, p. 306.

Makes 6 servings

1 4-pound piece Irish boiling bacon (see Sources, p. 21)
¼ cup (½ stick) butter
1 large head savoy cabbage, cored and sliced
Salt and pepper

1   Put the bacon in a large stewpot and cover with cold water. Bring to a boil over high heat. Reduce the heat and simmer for 1 hour, until the bacon is cooked through and tender when pierced with a knife tip.

2   Halfway through the cooking time, melt the butter in a large pot over medium heat. Add the cabbage leaves, turning to coat in the butter. Add 2 cups of water (if you like, add 2 cups of the bacon cooking water). Cover and cook for 20 minutes, stirring once or twice, until the cabbage is tender. Season with black pepper and salt as needed. Slice the bacon into thick pieces, about ¾-inch thick, and serve with the cabbage.

### MIND THE SALT

Irish bacon used to be sold very salty, and you were supposed to soak it overnight to leach out the worst of it. But these days, the bacon is usually sold less salty so you can skip the soaking step. In fact, if you soak the new lower-salt bacon, you may well end up with underseasoned meat that tastes oddly bland. When you're boiling the bacon, if a thick white scum appears on the surface, your bacon may be very salty. Let it boil for 30 minutes, then dump the water and start the bacon over in fresh water. The salt balance should be about right then.

# STEAK AND KIDNEY PIE

Fondly known as "Snake and Pygmy," in some ways the good old classic Steak and Kidney is a bit rich for today's tastes. When I was a kid though, it was one of my family's favorites and a frequent meal on cold, wet winter days. We would each be served a big gravy-sodden wedge of it with floury balls of potatoes and a heap of cooked cabbage. When I first left home, I regularly bought and ate the packaged variety, heating and eating it right out of the tin. But steak and kidney is still a luxurious meal, especially in winter. Ox or veal kidney is traditional, but I prefer the more delicate flavor and texture of lamb's kidneys. If you don't love kidneys, it's entirely acceptable to swap in mushrooms. You can also make the Beef and Oyster Stew on p. 77 and use that for the filling under the puff pastry, a modern trend that lightens up the old versions made with dense suet pastry.

Makes 6 to 8 servings

2 tablespoons cooking oil

1½ pounds well-marbled chuck, trimmed into 1-inch pieces

Salt and pepper

½ pound lamb's kidneys, cleaned and trimmed into 1-inch pieces

2 medium yellow onions, diced

2 medium carrots, diced

2 tablespoons butter

2 tablespoons flour

2 tablespoons tomato paste

4 cups beef stock (chicken stock is fine, too)

1 bay leaf

2 tablespoons Worcestershire sauce

8 ounces frozen puff pastry, thawed (one sheet from a 1-pound package)

1 egg

1   Put the oil in a large, deep skillet over medium-high heat. Sprinkle the cubed beef with salt and pepper. Fry in batches until well browned, transferring each batch to a platter.

2   Season the kidneys with salt and pepper and fry very quickly in the drippings left in the pan, just to brown them. Put them on top of the beef and set aside.

3   Melt the butter in the drippings left in the pan, and cook the onions and carrots over medium heat, stirring frequently, just until the onions are soft and lightly browned, 7 to 8 minutes.

4   Sprinkle the flour over the onion and carrot, and stir in the tomato paste. Slowly pour in the stock, stirring constantly to avoid lumps. Add the Worcestershire and the bay leaf, and return the steak and kidneys to the pan. Bring to a boil, reduce heat, and simmer gently for 1 ½ hours, until the beef is completely tender. If the mixture gets too dry, top up with a little more stock or water. Taste and adjust seasoning.

5   Preheat the oven to 400 degrees F and turn the mixture into a wide, shallow 2-quart baking dish. On a lightly floured surface, roll a sheet of pastry to ¼-inch thick. Trim it to be about 1 ½ inches larger all around than the dish. Lay the pastry on top, pushing it down the inside edges of the dish. With a sharp paring knife, cut several slits on top of the pastry.

6   Beat the egg with 1 tablespoon water and brush the surface of the pastry thickly with the egg. Bake for 35 to 40 minutes, until the pastry is puffed and golden and the pie is bubbling.

# COTTAGE *OR* SHEPHERD'S PIE

Not that long ago (say, 50 to 75 years ago—not long at all in a country that lives around and among the remains of Neolithic tombs), most kitchens had a grinder so they could process leftover bits of meat or make their own sausages. And a meat pie was the standard Monday dinner, made with the minced-up remains of the Sunday roast. If you'd had lamb, it was Shepherd's Pie. If you'd had beef, it was Cottage Pie. Happily, tastes have evolved, and nowadays we don't love re-cooked meat, but these quick meat pies are still a common supper dish; we just begin with uncooked ground lamb or ground beef. The leftover part is more likely the mashed potatoes, saved from a previous meal or two, and perhaps the veg—use a cup or two of whatever is already cooked and hanging around in the fridge. This is a straightforward, child-friendly recipe; if you want to dress it up a bit, tip a glass of red wine into the sauce along with the Worcestershire.

*Makes 6 servings*

1½ pounds ground beef or ground lamb
1 medium yellow onion, diced
1 large carrot, grated
1 teaspoon chopped fresh thyme leaves
2 tablespoons butter
2 tablespoons all-purpose flour
2 tablespoons tomato paste
1 cup beef stock
1 tablespoon Worcestershire sauce
Salt and pepper
1 cup green peas (cooked, fresh, or frozen, all are acceptable)
6 cups mashed potatoes
1 cup shredded cheddar cheese, optional

Shepherd's Pie with Buttered Turnip and Carrot, Kytelers Inn, Kilkenny, Ireland

1  Preheat the oven to 375 degrees F and lightly grease a 3-quart
   casserole dish.

2  Brown the beef in a large skillet over medium heat, 8 to 10 minutes.
   Spoon off and discard the excess fat. Push the meat to one side and
   cook the onion, carrot, and thyme for 5 to 6 minutes, until the onions
   are just turning translucent.

3  Push the onions and carrots to one side and melt the butter. Whisk
   the flour into the butter and then add in the tomato paste. Stir
   everything in the pan together. Add the stock and Worcestershire and
   cook for 5 to 7 minutes, until thickened. Season to taste with salt and
   a generous amount of pepper and then stir in the peas.

4  Turn the meat into the prepared dish and spoon the potatoes on top.
   Run the tip of a fork over the potatoes to make furrows and peaks
   so it will brown nicely. If desired, sprinkle cheese on top. Bake for 20
   minutes, until the meat is bubbling and the potatoes are browned.

# Of Mincing Machine and Majors

There's a line I've always loved from the Victorian authors Somerville
and Ross, who wrote the classic Irish R.M. series that's still very funny
and still very beloved in Ireland. Major Yeates, the hapless resident
magistrate who has moved to Ireland from Britain and is the butt
of all the locals' jokes as he strives to get along in his adopted land,
overhears the housekeeper exclaiming in tones of fury about the dog,
who had poached a hunk of roast beef off the table. "Sure he has it that
dhragged, that all we can do with it now is run  it through the mincing
machine for the Major's sandwiches."

Poultry at Bantry Market, Co. Cork

# POULTRY AND WILDFOWL

## 6

## To Souse a Turkey

Take a fat turkey and bone it and season it with pepper and salt and a good deal of mace and let it lie in that seasoning for a day or two, then draw the legs into the body tie it very tight in a cloth and boil it in salt and water then have ready your souse of salt and water with white wine vinegar, mace and pepper all boiled very well together so put your turkey into it.

—from an 18th century Irish cookbook manuscript

Pork products tend to elbow out chicken in popularity contests. I suppose there's only so much meat you can eat in a day. We do eat chicken, and Irish chicken is usually highly flavorful since many of our chickens are free-range. Many of the preparations are very simple, though: roasted chicken, or perhaps a chicken roasted with stuffing in it. One of the more luxurious preparations is Whiskey Chicken, which is sort of like Dublin Lawyer (p. 94) in its over-the-top decadence: the carved chicken waits, warm in its dish, while the pan juices are flamed with whiskey and finished with cream. Roast chicken never had it so good.

# CHICKEN AND HAM PIE

Nearly any stew-like filling can be put in a crust and called a pie, along the lines of Steak and Kidney Pie (p. 124), but Chicken and Ham is a particular favorite. The filling is mostly made up of moist pieces of chicken in a light, leek-scented, creamy sauce, and the pieces of ham add salt and savor to the dish. You can make a Chicken and Leek Pie by leaving out the ham and doubling the quantity of leeks.

*Makes 6 servings*

¼ cup (½ stick) butter

¼ cup all-purpose flour

1 large leek, white and green parts, thinly sliced and washed

2 cups chicken stock

1 cup light cream

2 ½ cups diced, cooked chicken

1 cup diced, cooked ham

1 cup peas, canned or frozen

2 tablespoons minced fresh flat-leaf parsley

Salt and pepper

1 sheet frozen pastry (puff or shortcrust), thawed

1 egg

1   Preheat the oven to 400 degrees F and lightly butter a large, deep-dish 9-inch pie plate.

2   In a large saucepan over medium heat, melt the butter. Add the leek slices, tossing to coat. Cover the pan and cook for 10 minutes, until the leek is tender but not browned. Gradually pour in the chicken stock, stirring all the time to prevent lumps. Add the light cream and bring to a gentle simmer. Add the chicken, ham, peas, and parsley. Cook for 3 to 4 minutes, until thickened slightly. Season with salt and pepper, and spoon into the prepared pie dish.

3   Roll the pastry out and cut into a circle about 12 inches in diameter, so there's plenty of overhang on the pie plate. Lift the pastry on top of the pie and tuck the overhang down the inside rim.

4   Use a sharp paring knife to cut slits in the top of the pie. Beat the egg with 1 tablespoon water and brush this glaze on top of the pastry. Bake for 20 minutes, until pastry is golden and the pie is bubbling.

## DINNER-PLATE CHICKEN PIES

You can use the filling from the Chicken and Ham Pie to make an old-fashioned dinner-plate pie. Use the pastry for the Apple Tart on p. 238 and roll it out to line a deep, ovenproof dinner plate with a slanted rim. Put in 1 cup or so of the filling, just enough to fill the bottom of the dinner plate but not to risk overflowing. Roll out a second crust and top the pie. Pinch the edges together firmly, or use a fork to seal. Cut several slits in the top and brush with egg. Bake for 25 minutes at 350 degrees F until the crust is browned. Depending on the size of your plate, you can make as many dinner-plate pies as you have diners, or you can divide one among two or three people if your plates are large. The point of dinner-plate pies was to stretch a serving of meat with more crust than filling. They can be savory or sweet. One of my favorite childhood desserts was a dinner-plate apple pie, with a thin layer of sweetened apples and a lot of tender browned pastry.

# MUSTARD ROASTED CHICKEN

Irish butcher shops are full of whole chickens, jointed chickens, breasts on the bone or off; any sort of part that you want is readily available. So I love an all-purpose chicken recipe that lets me take advantage of whatever pieces look plumpest and freshest—or are on sale for the best price. In Ireland, I make this mustard-baked chicken with a coarse, whole-grain mustard blended with whiskey that is readily available there, but it's easily replicated. Use any mustard that you like, but something with a bit of a kick: Dijon, spicy brown, or any coarse- or whole-grain mustard. The whiskey is not strictly necessary but it adds a warm, almost meaty flavor in the background—it's the Irish *umami*, whiskey, our fifth taste (after sweet, salty, sour, bitter) and the savor that we enjoy in all sorts of unlikely foods, whether it's whipped cream, porridge, or marmalade. Or chicken, as here. I use parsley but this all-purpose recipe will readily accommodate any cut of chicken, any kind of mustard, and any herb (tarragon is especially good). Butter ties it all together, but a drizzle of cream would do the same job.

Makes 4 servings

4 chicken breasts (on the bone)
Salt and pepper
1/3 cup coarse-grain mustard
3 tablespoons chopped fresh parsley
3 tablespoons whiskey
4 tablespoons butter (plus more for greasing)

1   Preheat oven to 375 degrees F and butter a baking dish. Spread the chicken pieces out in the dish, just touching, and sprinkle it with salt and pepper.

2   In a small dish, combine the mustard, whiskey, and parsley. Smear it all over the top of each piece of chicken and dot the chicken with the butter.

3   Cover the dish tightly with foil and bake for about 30 minutes. Remove the foil and continue to cook for another 15 to 20 minutes, until the chicken is browned and tender. (Cooking times may vary depending on what pieces of chicken you use.)

# WHISKEY CHICKEN

A chicken is roasted with butter until the skin is crisp. Then the pan juices are flambéed with whiskey, and cream is added to the sauce. It's the richest roast chicken imaginable, a treat for a special occasion. If you're not used to flaming food with alcohol, don't be afraid—just be prepared to stay well back. When you add the whiskey to the hot pan, it takes a moment for the cold alcohol to heat up and be ready to flame, but in a few moments, once it's hot, it will readily catch fire, either with a match held to the side of the pan or by tipping the pan slightly toward the gas flame of the stovetop. The whiskey lights with a whoosh! So don't be leaning forward over the pan. You'll see it catch fire, and then it burns out brightly and quickly. It's a spectacle, it's very fun, and the purpose is to burn off the harsh taste of the alcohol and leave only the flavor behind. This dish is so rich you don't need much alongside it. Try a green salad and some bread to sop up the excellent juices. Use a smallish chicken; if it's too big, the meat can be tough. If you need to serve more people, it's better to roast two smaller chickens than one big one.

Makes 4 servings
1 2- to 2 ½-pound chicken
¼ cup (½ stick) butter, softened
Salt and pepper
1 lemon
3 tablespoons whiskey
½ cup heavy cream

1  Preheat the oven to 400 degrees F. Rub the chicken all over with the softened butter and squeeze the two lemon halves over it. Put the squeezed lemons inside the chicken's cavity and sprinkle the bird liberally with salt and pepper, inside and out.

2  Put the chicken in a cast-iron skillet or roasting pan, and roast until golden brown and crisp, about 1 hour, or until an instant-read thermometer poked in the thickest part of the thigh reads 180 degrees F.

3  Carve the chicken and place it on a warm serving platter. Set aside to stay warm. Spoon off and discard the visible fat from the roasting pan or cast-iron skillet. Set the pan over medium heat and pour the whiskey into the pan. Let it heat for a moment, then either set a match to the edge of the pan, or, if you have a gas stove, tilt the pan away from you toward the gas flame. The warmed whiskey will light and burn out quickly. (If the burning makes you anxious, clap on a tight-fitting lid.)

4  Pour in the cream and heat through, stirring to scrape up any browned bits from the bottom of the pan. Pour the sauce over the carved chicken and serve at once.

# CHICKEN AND FRUIT CURRY

We do have a taste for a little sweetness with our meat in Ireland and that extends even to curried chicken. This version has a little soft fruit in it. I like peaches, but you could use plums, apricots, pineapple pieces, or a few chunks of ripe pear. If you prefer, skip the fruit. But we do like a mild curry: we don't go in for the blistering hot vindaloo curries that are so loved in the UK. Still, curry is a dish that regularly pops up on supper tables because it's warm, and comforting, and quick. This recipe starts with raw chicken, but if you pull the meat off a rotisserie chicken and cut it into bite-size pieces, you can skip cooking the chicken and just add the meat to the finished sauce in step 3 to heat through. Serve over rice.

*Makes 4 servings*

**3 tablespoons cooking oil**
**3 boneless, skinless chicken breasts, cut into 1-inch pieces**
**1 large onion, thinly sliced**
**1 2-inch piece ginger, finely chopped**
**2 garlic cloves, minced**
**3 tablespoons mild curry paste (or to taste)**
**1 14-ounce container coconut milk**
**2 ripe, medium peaches, peeled and cut into chunks**

1 In a large skillet over medium heat, place the cooking oil and cook the chicken pieces until lightly browned, 6 to 7 minutes. With a slotted spoon, lift the chicken into a bowl and set aside.

2 Put the onion into the fat remaining in the pan and cook over medium heat for 6 to 7 minutes, until the onion is softened and lightly browned. Add the ginger and garlic and cook for a minute. Stir the curry paste into the pan and cook for 1 to 2 minutes.

3 Blend in the coconut milk, a little at a time. Bring the coconut milk to a boil. Reduce the heat and return the chicken to the pan. Simmer for 5 minutes to cook the chicken through. Add the peaches and continue cooking for 5 minutes or so to thicken the sauce slightly.

# HERB-STUFFED ROAST CHICKEN

Thyme and parsley are so necessary to the Irish kitchen that in many grocery stores, you can buy a package marked "Herbs" that consists of a bunch of parsley and a tangle of thyme. Together, the two are just about all you need to make a fragrant herb stuffing for roast chicken, but I like to supplement with some sage as well. An old saying holds that the fortunes of the household are mirrored by how well the sage in your garden is growing, so I try to take good care of the pot of sage in my windowsill!

We don't like too much or too thick of a gravy, and this version takes advantage of the pan juices without being too rich or fatty.

*Makes 4 servings*

1 2 ½- to 3-pound chicken
¼ cup (½ stick) butter, softened
Salt and pepper
1 small yellow onion, diced
2 cups soft breadcrumbs
½ cup chopped fresh parsley
1 tablespoon fresh thyme leaves, chopped
1 tablespoon chopped fresh sage leaves
1 ¼ cups chicken stock
1 tablespoon all-purpose flour

1 Preheat the oven to 400 degrees F. Rub the chicken all over with two tablespoons of the softened butter, and salt and pepper it inside and out.

2 In a cast-iron or other ovenproof skillet over medium heat, melt the remaining butter and cook the onion until just softened and barely browned, 5 to 6 minutes. Turn off the heat and stir in the breadcrumbs and herbs. Pour ¼ cup of the chicken stock over all, and stir to make a moist stuffing. Pack it into the chicken's cavity. Wipe out the skillet with a paper towel and set the chicken in the skillet.

3 Roast for 60 to 70 minutes, until the stuffing in the center registers 165 degrees F on an instant-read thermometer and the thickest part of the thigh registers 180 degrees F. Lift the chicken onto a serving platter and put the skillet over medium heat. Stir the flour into the juices, scraping up the browned bits as you stir. Slowly mix in the remaining cup of chicken stock, and bring to a boil just to thicken. Season with salt and pepper.

4 Carve the chicken and serve each portion with a spoonful of the stuffing and some gravy.

# HOLIDAY TURKEY WITH SAUSAGE STUFFING

Irish turkeys are generally smaller than American ones. A breed called the Bronze are the preferred turkeys in Ireland, and they're not overly processed nor overly large. They usually come with head and feet attached so you can see the quality of the bird and be sure you know what you're getting. Also, you could hang them by the feet. My dad always left the Christmas turkey hanging in the coldest part of our pantry for the week before Christmas, which made it more tender and intensified the flavor. Look for a smaller, organic turkey—12 pounds is about as big as you want for best flavor. Rub it all over with lemony butter, and stuff only the neck cavity, not the body. Then it won't take as long to cook.

Makes 8 to 10 servings

For the stuffing:

2 tablespoons butter

8 ounces Irish sausage (p. 000), casing removed

1 large yellow onion, diced

2 celery stalks, sliced thin

4 cups breadcrumbs

½ cup chopped fresh parsley

2 tablespoons chopped fresh sage

½ cup chicken stock

Salt and pepper

For the turkey:

½ cup unsalted butter, softened

Zest and juice of 1 lemon

1 (12-pound) whole turkey

Salt and pepper

1   Preheat the oven to 350 degrees F. To make the stuffing, melt the butter in a large skillet over medium heat and cook the sausage, breaking it up with a spoon. Add the onion and celery and continue to cook until the onion is tender. Stir in the breadcrumbs and herbs and moisten with chicken stock. Taste and season with salt and pepper as needed.

2   In a medium bowl, stir together the softened butter with the lemon zest and juice. (Once you've squeezed the lemon halves, toss them into the turkey's main cavity.) Rub the lemon butter mixture all over the turkey, above and beneath the skin. Season the turkey liberally with salt and pepper, inside the cavity and out.

3   Pack the stuffing into the neck cavity and fold the flap of skin over it. Secure the skin in place with a skewer or toothpick. Set the turkey on a rack in a roasting pan and cover loosely with foil. Pour two cups of water into the roasting pan.

4   Roast 3 to 3 ½ hours, until an instant-read thermometer in the breast reads 165 degrees F and the thickest part of the thigh registers 180 degrees F. For the last hour, remove the foil so the breast can brown. Remove the turkey from the oven and tent it again with foil while it rests for at least 15 and up to 30 minutes before carving.

Vegetable Stall, Howth Sunday Market

# ROAST PHEASANT WITH APPLES AND CREAM

Pheasant was once very much a seasonal food. In the late autumn, walking down Moore Street, along the market street of central Dublin, there would be braces of pheasant hanging in the windows of the many butcher shops that lined the street. Now pheasant is raised for food so it's not the same rare indulgence it once was, but it's still a treat. It's typically served with red cabbage, which complements the gamey flavor beautifully.

*Makes 4 servings*
**2 dressed pheasants**
**½ cup (1 stick) butter, softened**
**Salt and pepper**
**6 tart cooking apples, peeled and sliced thinly**
**1 cup heavy cream**
**1 cup apple cider**

1   Preheat the oven to 375 degrees F. Rub the pheasants with half the butter and sprinkle salt and pepper inside and outside the pheasants.

2   In a large, ovenproof skillet over medium heat, melt the remaining butter, and cook the apples until softened. Lay the pheasants on top of the apples, spooning some of the apples over and around the pheasants. Drizzle them with the cider, then with cream.

3   Roast the pheasants for 45 to 55 minutes, until an instant-read thermometer inserted in the breast reads 145 degrees F.

4   Lift the pheasants onto a warmed serving dish, and use a slotted spoon to spoon the apples around them. Drizzle the juices over all and serve at once.

## 7

# VEGETABLES AND SIDE DISHES

## To Keep French Beans

Take the red kidney bean (the white will not keep) lay a layer of beans and a layer of salt in a crock till full put suet a top to keep out the air, small pots are best for that reason, when you dress your beans cut them longways like chips and lay them in warm water to take out the salt change the water two or three times it will make them green and fresh boil them as usual.

—from an 18th century Irish cookbook manuscript

Here's a brief tale that will illustrate better than anything else how the Irish feel about potatoes: To understand it, you must first know the French pride themselves, as with so many other of their food, on the quality of their potatoes, and they are exquisite. I can buy expensive French fingerling potatoes, such as *rattes*, at gourmet stores and greenmarkets at a huge markup in New York. And yet, when my parents used to own a house in France where they stayed for long months every summer, they took along enough potatoes to last them all summer. As much as they loved France, and the food, and the wine, there was simply no negotiating when it came to potatoes. Proper Irish potatoes, or nothing.

As I've mentioned elsewhere, the key characteristic is flouriness, no matter what you're doing to them. In America, the best bet is probably a russet. When we want a waxier potato, we call it a new potato, and we eat it with butter and mint as a rite to herald the arrival of spring.

In the same way Eskimos are supposed to have countless words for snow, we have countless things you can do to a potato, and I'll give you the major recipes and a few of the quirkier ones. But what other vegetables do we eat? Cabbage, carrots, cauliflower, leeks and onions, kale and Brussels sprouts, celery and parsnips, turnips and rutabagas, lined up roughly in order of popularity. If you told most Irish people they could never have any other vegetable again besides these—and potatoes, obviously—most of them would look at you blankly: What other vegetables are there?

# BRASSICAS

KALE
BROCCOLI
TURNIP
RADISH
BRUSSEL SPROUT
LETTUCE
CORIANDER
BASIL

# COLCANNON

Halloween is actually an Irish holiday. Called Samhain (SOW-ann) in ancient Celtic tradition, it's the traditional autumn festival when the spirits of the dead walk the earth. Translated to the Christian era from the pagan, it became All Hallow's Eve, the night before All Saint's Day. Thus the spirits and the jack-o'-lanterns carried from one tradition to the next. Turnips used to be carved out and lit to frighten away unwanted interaction between the living and dead on the long dark roads. The Irish still have unlit roads throughout the country, but people don't walk them with carved turnips. They do, however, still eat the traditional foods of Halloween—barmbrack (p. 195) and colcannon. In the Catholic tradition, All Hallow's Eve was a fast day, meaning no meat, but this supper of potatoes mashed with butter and cream, scallions, and chopped kale, was warming and satisfying. It's traditionally served in a huge mound, a festive meal eaten communally, with a pool of melted butter in the center for dipping. For Halloween, a coin, a button, a ring, and a thimble were hidden in the colcannon. Whoever found one received, respectively, wealth, bachelorhood, marriage, or spinsterhood in the coming year.

*Makes 4 servings*
**8 large russet potatoes**
**1 pound curly kale**
**Salt**
**1 cup half and half (or whole milk)**
**1 bunch scallions, green parts only, chopped**
**2 tablespoons butter (and more for serving)**
**Freshly ground white pepper**

1   Peel and quarter the potatoes and place in a saucepan. Fill with cold water to cover and add a teaspoon of salt. Simmer until potatoes are tender, about 20 minutes.

2   While the potatoes are cooking, bring a second pot of salted water to a boil. Strip the kale from the tough center ribs and discard the ribs. Chop the kale coarsely and cook in the boiling water until tender, about 15 minutes. Drain, and when it's cool enough to handle, chop it very finely.

3   In a small saucepan, heat the half-and-half or milk until hot, not boiling. Stir in the chopped scallions and the butter.

4   Mash the potatoes, stirring in the half-and-half.

> **GREEN STUFF**
> Although the name colcannon originally comes from the Irish cal ciann fhionn, meaning white-headed cabbage, it has been made all over Ireland for generations using dark green curly kale, never cabbage. In Ireland, curly kale shows up in stores in the autumn, right around Halloween.

## New Potatoes with Mint

How can new potatoes herald the arrival of spring? Our winters are generally quite temperate: the first daffodils push up in mid-February, and the first tiny potatoes are ready to be harvested about a month after that. They're always eaten boiled, sometimes with butter and salt, but usually like this:

Boil new potatoes in cold, salted water until tender, about 10 minutes. Drain the potatoes, leaving just a tablespoon or so of the cooking water in the pot. Drop in a big lump of butter and a handful of thinly sliced fresh mint leaves. Cover with the pot's lid, and holding the lid down firmly with a dish towel or potholder, shake the pot firmly up and down and side to side. The butter, mint, and cooking water will emulsify into a sort of sauce on the slightly bruised and bumped up potatoes, whose skins will crack during the shaking to absorb the sauce. Eat at once.

# ROAST POTATOES

If you've ever eaten at an Irish hotel, you probably had some potatoes on the plate with a sort of leathery, brown skin. Those were meant to be roasted potatoes, parboiled and baked with fat until they're crisped and browned. But roast potatoes famously do not hold up well, so hotel versions, even at good restaurants, are usually a disappointment. This is a treat best made at home.

We call them "roasties," and they're either a special-occasion treat or an everyday occurrence, depending on the patience of who does the cooking at your house. People take their roasties very seriously, and there's a trick to getting them just right. One of those tricks is goose fat, which some families stockpile from the holiday bird and save all year. (It will stay fresh in the refrigerator for months.) The other is parboiling to just the right point. We have a name for roasties that are boiled too long: Mashed Potatoes.

To make good roasties, peel as many medium-sized, floury potatoes as you want. Larger potatoes should be halved. The ideal size is a sort of medium, oval potato: not too big, not too small or round like a new potato. The oven is presumably already blazing away, roasting your joint or bird, but if not, preheat it to about 400 degrees F. Place potatoes in cold, salted water and boil for about 15 minutes, until the potato is not quite cooked. A knife can't push to the center with total ease. You sort of have to try it a few times and develop a feel for it.

Drain the parboiled potatoes and let them dry out for a couple minutes.

Some people preheat a baking dish with oil in it. I heat oil in a very large cast-iron skillet on the stovetop. But whatever method you prefer, don't put potatoes in cold oil for roasties.

Here's how I do it: Heat a large, heavy, ovenproof skillet on the stovetop for several minutes. Ladle about 1/4 inch of fat (goose, duck, beef), peanut oil, or olive oil in the bottom. Let the fat or oil heat in the skillet for a couple minutes. Add the potatoes and gently ladle the hot fat over each one. Don't toss them vigorously, or you'll break up the potatoes.

Sprinkle lightly with salt. Place in the oven and bake for 45 to 60 minutes, shaking the pan now and then. Roasties can be forgiving enough to stay in the oven another 20 to 30 minutes if your roast isn't done yet, but no longer. They should be very crispy and dark brown all over. Keeping them warm for more than an hour will result in that leathery hotel skin.

# BOXTY

Combining cooked and raw potato with flour to make a thick cake is a decidedly northern recipe. It's very common throughout Ulster, and we're aware of it and occasionally run across it in other parts of Ireland, the same way, you might say, that parts of America know other parts of America eat a lot of barbecue, even though you might not eat it every day. There is in Dublin a restaurant of many years standing called The Boxty House, where large, flat boxty cakes are rolled around a variety of fillings such as creamed bacon and cabbage.

1 large potato
2 cups all-purpose flour, plus more for kneading
1 cup leftover mashed potatoes
½ cup (1 stick) butter
1 teaspoon baking powder
1 teaspoon salt
2 to 3 tablespoons whole milk

1   Grate the raw potato directly into a bowl. Lift the pieces and squeeze them into the bowl with your hands, setting the squeezed shreds aside on a small plate. You're trying to get as much liquid out as possible. Let the liquid in the bowl settle, then pour the thin juice off the dense starch that will settle to the bottom. Discard the juice and return the shreds to the bowl.

2   Stir in the flour, mashed potato, and butter right away to prevent the grated potato from discoloring. Add the baking powder and salt, and turn the mixture out onto a lightly floured work surface. Knead gently, just to combine. If the dough is very stiff and dry, knead in a couple tablespoons milk.

3   Divide the dough into quarters. Pat each piece into a large circle about ½-inch thick. If you're filling them, leave them whole, but if you're eating them the traditional way, use a knife to score each circle with a cross, cutting not quite through the dough.

4   Heat a cast-iron skillet over medium heat. With a large spatula, lift each boxty into the pan. Cook on each side until golden brown, 5 to 6 minutes per side. Eat hot, with butter.

# CHAMP (CALLY)

Mashed potatoes with hot milk, butter, and scallions, or green onions, as we call them in Ireland, is what Dubliners call Champ. But my mother is from the west of Ireland, and she always refers to this dish as Cally. When we make plain mashed potatoes, with a little butter, milk, and salt and pepper, we like them quite stiff and dry. But when we make Champ, they should be softer and looser. It's typically served with a good dollop of butter on top of each person's mound of potatoes, and in country families, a filling plate of cally might serve as your entire evening meal.

*Makes 4 to 6 servings*
**8 large russet potatoes, peeled**
**¾ cup whole milk**
**¼ cup (½ stick) butter, plus more for serving**
**1 bunch scallions**
**Salt and pepper**

1  Halve or quarter the potatoes if they're very large. Put them in a large saucepan and cover with cold, salted water. Bring to a boil over medium-high heat, reduce the heat slightly, and simmer the potatoes until tender, 12 to 15 minutes. Drain well and shake the drained potatoes in the pan over the heat for a moment to dry them out.

2  Before the potatoes finish cooking, heat the milk and butter together in a small saucepan. Slice the scallions, green and white parts, thinly. Turn this mixture into the milk and heat through, just to soften the scallions slightly.

3  Mash the potatoes with a masher and slowly blend in the milk mixture. You may not need quite all the milk. Beat the potatoes with a fork or a large wooden spoon to make them fluffy. The potatoes should be soft but not too loose; they should still be able to form a peak so they can be mounded on serving plates. Season well with salt and pepper.

4  To serve, heap up a portion of champ on a plate, make a dent in the top of the mound and drop in a dollop of butter to melt into the indentation.

# Praties in the Kettle

Growing up in Dublin, I often spent summers on Inisheer, the smallest of the three Aran Islands off the coast of Galway. This counted as summer camp for Irish kids. We were distributed, several teens to a house, among the island residents, and we spent our days roaming the island, practicing our Irish vocabulary, and listening to local musicians at night. But one of the things I remember most vividly is how the *bean an tí* (bahn ahn tee—literally "woman of the house" and the sole name we all used to address our hostesses) cooked.

In the cottage where I stayed, the bean an tí had two cast-iron kettles in her kitchen, and not much more. The small cast-iron kettle was known as a bastible. It had legs to stand in the fire and a close-fitting lid. She'd put it in the fireplace and heap coals on the lid to bake the soda bread. The larger one served to boil the mountains of potatoes that, along with fish, made up our diet.

She always fed us before the *fear an tí* (far ahn tee, "the man of the house") came home from fishing, and she boiled our potatoes on the stovetop. The man of the house, however, preferred the taste of potatoes cooked in cast iron over a peat fire, so when he came home after his day's labors on the waves, the woman of the house lugged that heavy kettle over to the fire to provide that smokey turf fire flavor for him.

# CHIVE POTATO SALAD

This potato salad looks extremely simple (okay, I'll just say it: plain) compared to American potato salads full of mustard, vinegar, dill pickles, eggs, and so on. But it has a surprisingly robust character that highlights the flavor of the potato, so this is a great recipe to show off distinctive heirloom potatoes or pricey fingerlings. Don't skimp on the chives. An entire bunch is necessary to bring out their gentle savor.

Though the Irish love floury potatoes, fluffy, floury spuds tend to break apart when boiling and can fall into mush when stirred up as a potato salad. Be sure to use a waxier boiling potato for this salad, such as Red Bliss or a multi-purpose potato such as Yukon Gold.

*Makes 4 servings*
1½ pounds boiling potatoes, scrubbed, skins on, halved
½ cup mayonnaise
1 bunch fresh chives, chopped in pieces about ½-inch long
 (about ¾ cup chopped)
Salt and freshly ground black pepper
Juice of 1 lemon

1 Cook the potatoes until tender. Drain and cool in large glass bowl. When the potatoes are cool enough to handle, cut them into bite-size pieces. Remove any large pieces of skin that slip off as you work, but pieces of skin that cling to the potato should remain.

2 In a small bowl, stir together the mayonnaise, chives, salt, pepper, and lemon juice. Pour over the potatoes and stir gently to combine. Chill until ready to serve.

# SPRING CABBAGE

As I have mentioned elsewhere, in Ireland the cabbage we eat so much of is not the greeny-white heads of tightly packed cabbage found in America. Instead, our typical cabbage is early-season spring cabbage: big, long, loose bunches of heavy, dark-green leaves. York cabbage is a popular variety of spring cabbage, and while you will see cabbage in Irish markets throughout the year, the best, freshest, sweetest bunches appear in the early spring. I've never come across Irish spring cabbage in America, but I get good results by substituting milder savoy cabbage, which is somewhat similar to spring cabbage in shape and size, and adding a little kale for color and flavor.

*Makes 6 servings*
**3 tablespoons butter**
**1 pound savoy cabbage, cored and chopped**
**½ pound kale (1 small bunch), stems discarded, roughly chopped**
**Salt and pepper**

1   In a large pot over medium heat, melt the butter. When it foams, add the chopped kale and toss to coat. Pour in a cup of water and clap on the lid. Bring to a boil and cook, 5 to 7 minutes, until the leaves are softened.

2   Add the savoy cabbage and stir it in well. Put the lid back on and cook another 6 to 7 minutes, just until the leaves are tender but still toothsome, not mushy. Season liberally with salt and plenty of black pepper. Eat hot.

# MASHED CARROTS AND PARSNIPS

Coarsely mashing boiled carrots and parsnips together with a little
butter highlights the sweetness of both. The two vegetables will not fully
incorporate completely into a pale orange mash, but instead the orange and
white parts stay just separate enough to make a beautiful mosaic. Alongside
a heap of dark-green spring cabbage, it's an Irish flag on a plate.

*Makes 6 serving*
**1 pound carrots (3 to 4 large)**
**1 pound parsnips (about 4 to 6 medium)**
**Salt and pepper**
**2 to 3 tablespoons butter**

1   Peel and dice the carrots and parsnips. Put in a saucepan with
    cold, salted water just to cover. Bring to a boil, then reduce heat
    and simmer gently until the vegetables are completely tender,
    15 to 20 minutes. (Test them once or twice with a fork.)

2   Drain and add the butter to the pot. Mash with a potato masher
    to a coarse purèe, and season with plenty of salt and black pepper.

## Glazed Carrots

The sort of sugar or maple-glazed cooked carrots you sometimes see in
America are uncommon in Ireland. If Americans can be said to have a sweet
tooth, I think it's only fair to say the Irish have a butter-and-cream tooth!
Root vegetables tend to be pretty sweet on their own, so we just glaze them
with liberal amounts of butter, or sometimes a cream sauce. For glazed
carrots, cut peeled carrots into thin slices on the diagonal, and simmer in
salted water until tender. Drain and add enough butter to give them a sheen.
Remember large carrots tend to be sweeter than their smaller, skinnier
counterparts.

# BRAISED CELERY AND CARROTS IN BUTTER SAUCE

I wonder if it's because our weather is so raw already that we don't eat much in the way of raw vegetables. The way the American kids eat raw celery and carrot sticks, Irish kids will eat cooked celery and carrot slices, often floating in a slightly thickened butter sauce. The celery should be cut in slightly bigger pieces than the carrots, so they cook evenly. It's common to make this dish with something very simple, such as boiled potatoes and roast chicken, so the sauce on the vegetables serves as a sort of overall gravy for the plate. I simmer the vegetables entirely in chicken stock, to infuse them with more flavor, but you can also simmer them in salted water until tender, then drain them and make the sauce as below but using 1 ½ cups chicken stock.

Makes 6 servings

**1 pound carrots (3 to 4 large)**
**1 pound celery (4 to 5 stalks)**
**3 cups chicken stock**
**3 tablespoons butter, softened**
**3 tablespoons flour**
**Salt and pepper**

1   Peel the carrots and cut into 1/4-inch slices on the diagonal. Cut the celery into ½-inch pieces. Place in a saucepan and cover with the chicken stock. Bring to a boil, reduce heat, cover loosely, and simmer gently for 15 to 20 minutes, until the vegetables are completely tender when pierced with a knife.

2   While the vegetables are cooking, in a small plate or bowl, cream the softened butter with the flour using a fork or the back of a spoon.

3   When the vegetables are tender, some of the stock will have evaporated. Drop nuggets of the butter-flour mixture into the bubbling liquid and stir to combine. Watch as you stir; if the sauce starts to thicken to your liking, you may not need the entire amount of butter and flour. You want a thick sauce with a buttery sheen, but still liquid enough to flow like gravy, not a dense paste. Season with salt, if needed, and lots of black pepper.

# MASHED TURNIPS (OR RUTABAGA)

In Ireland, when we make mashed turnips, it's nearly always mashed rutabaga. Actual turnips are the little, watery-fleshed, sweet, white and pink root vegetables we roast or boil and eat in spring. But the meatier, starchier veg we call "turnip" is the big, starchy, yellow-fleshed vegetable Americans mostly think of as rutabagas. They usually come thickly waxed, and there's a band of dark purple around the stem end. They are tough to peel with a vegetable peeler. It's easier to cut the stem end off level, then turn the rutabaga upside down on a cutting board, and carefully sawing downward as you work your way around, cut the waxed skin off in big peels with a sharp chef's knife.

*Makes 4 servings*
**1 large rutabaga**
**2 to 3 tablespoons butter**
**Salt and pepper**

1   Peel the rutabaga and cut into 1-inch cubes. Put in a saucepan and cover with salted water. Bring to a boil over medium-high heat, reduce heat, and simmer until tender. This may take as little as 15 minutes, or as long as 25 minutes, depending on the age of your rutabaga. Check it occasionally with the tip of a paring knife to see if it's tender.

2   Drain well and add as much butter as you can bear—even 4 tablespoons, if you like. Mash with a potato masher and then whip with a fork to make them fluffy. Season with a little salt, if needed, and a lot of black pepper. The pepper's bite is delicious against the sweet, buttery flesh.

# CAULIFLOWER CHEESE

When I was a child, the words "Cauliflower Cheese" struck horror into me at dinnertime, mainly because my mother's occasionally over-frugal ways meant it was simply a boiled cauliflower covered in a lumpy white sauce of far more flour than cheese. I have since gone on to a much more successful career in cauliflower and cheese, so that my older son greets this dish at supper with cries of joy. White pepper is common, because it adds a sharper flavor to the sauce, but black pepper is fine, too.

*Makes 6 servings*
1 large head cauliflower
2 tablespoons butter
2 tablespoons flour
1½ cups whole milk
8 ounces sharp cheddar cheese (preferably white cheddar)
¼ teaspoon freshly grated nutmeg
Salt and black or white pepper

1 Preheat the oven to 375 degrees F and butter a 1-quart shallow casserole dish. Break the cauliflower into florets and boil or steam until tender, 10 to 15 minutes. (I like to steam it because then the cauliflower is not waterlogged and tastes cheesier.)

2 In a medium saucepan over medium heat, melt the butter and stir in the flour. Pour the milk slowly in, whisking constantly, to avoid lumps. Bring the milk just to a simmer, stirring frequently, and cook 2 to 3 minutes, until the sauce thickens.

3 Add the cheese by handfuls, reserving one last handful. Stir until melted. Season with nutmeg, salt, and plenty of pepper.

4 Spread the cooked cauliflower florets evenly in the prepared casserole dish and pour the cheese sauce over all. Sprinkle the reserved handful of cheese over the top. Bake for 10 minutes, until the casserole is bubbling and lightly browned in spots.

# BRAISED FENNEL

When my wife and I were dating—she was an American student in Dublin at the time—we used to often cook elaborate meals together, drinking a glass of wine or two as we worked. Now, dinner preparation begins with one of us saying frantically, "Who's making dinner?! Quick! The kids are starving!" But back in the day, during one of our leisurely courtship rituals, I was involved in something complicated—I don't recall, wrapping a beef tenderloin in pastry or something else I'd never do now—while she looked on and sipped from her glass. Distracted, I said to her rather sharply, "Haven't you prepped that fennel yet? This is going to be done soon!" and she said to me, helplessly looking around the kitchen, "But...I don't know what fennel is!" We've come a long way.

Makes 4 servings

2 large fennel bulbs
2 tablespoons butter
1½ cups chicken stock
Salt and pepper

1  Prepare the fennel by trimming off the protruding fronds and stems, leaving only the solid bulb, which is sort of ribbed like celery. Trim off the root end, leaving a flat base, and then, cutting downward, quarter each bulb.

2  Slice each quarter into thin pieces lengthwise. The fennel bulb will naturally fall into segments, so trim it just to make sure the pieces are all a similar size.

3  In a large skillet, melt the butter over medium heat. Add the fennel and toss to coat. Stir and cook for 3 to 4 minutes to let the fennel pieces brown a little. Pour on the chicken stock, cover, and simmer gently for 15 minutes, until the fennel is tender.

4  Remove the lid, raise the heat slightly if necessary, and simmer to reduce the stock to a light syrupy glaze. Taste and season with salt, if needed, and plenty of black pepper.

# LEEK AND CHEESE PIE

Meatless meals on Friday were once extremely important in Ireland, as the Catholic Church considered Friday a fasting day, requiring some sort of penance, such as abstaining from meat. (Although Ireland remains a mostly Catholic country, the practice has largely died out.) This leek and cheese pie, bolstered with potatoes, is in the style of filling vegetarian dishes that might constitute dinner on a meatless Friday. Skipping the crust makes it an elegant and elaborate side dish for a festive meal and helps highlight the leeks' delicate flavor. Americans tend to use leeks mainly for soup, but in Ireland they're a more multi-purpose vegetable, whether braised, baked, boiled, roasted as a vegetable to accompany roast meats, or incorporated into other dishes.

Makes 4 servings

For the pastry:

2 cups all-purpose flour
1 teaspoon salt
8 tablespoons (1 stick) cold butter
1 large egg, divided into white and yolk
1 tablespoon cold water

For the filling:

2 medium baking potatoes
6 large leeks, green parts removed, sliced into ⅛-inch rounds and washed well in cold water

2 tablespoons butter
2 tablespoons flour
1½ cups milk
2 cups grated sharp cheddar
¼ teaspoon grated nutmeg
Salt and freshly ground black pepper

1   Make the pastry combining the flour and salt in a food processor. Cut the butter into 8 pieces and pulse until mixture resembles fine cornmeal. Add the egg yolk (reserving the white) and 1 tablespoon cold water and process until the mixture forms a ball. If you need more water, add it 1 teaspoon at a time.  Wrap the dough in plastic wrap and place in the freezer for ½ hour, or in the refrigerator for up to 2 days.

2   To make the filling, peel the potatoes and cut them into bite-size pieces. Cook in salted water until tender, then drain, reserving ½ cup of the cooking water.

3   Preheat the oven to 350 degrees F. Sauté the leeks in butter until softened, then sprinkle on the flour and stir well. Stir in the milk slowly and cook until sauce thickens. Add the cheese and stir over medium heat until melted. Season with nutmeg, salt, and pepper to taste.

4    Stir in the cooked, drained potatoes and a couple tablespoons of the potato cooking water so the mixture isn't too thick. (Add more if it looks very thick. The leeks and potatoes should be saucy.)

5    Roll out half the pastry and fit it into a deep-dish, 8-inch pie pan. Spoon in the leek mixture. Roll out the remaining pastry and cover the top of the pastry, crimping the edges with a fork.

6    Cut several long slits in the top, crust, and brush all over with the reserved egg white. Bake for 50-60 minutes, until the crust is golden brown and the sauce is bubbling through the slits. (If the edges brown before the sauce is bubbling, cover the edges with aluminum foil.)

RUB IT IN

Food processors make pastry incredibly simple. It's much easier to cut shortening into flour with a high-speed blade rather than the labor-intensive work of cutting it with two knives or a fork. Irish recipes for pastry never say to "cut" in the butter, however; they usually say to "rub" in the butter. My wife asked me about that early in our marriage and I was surprised. "You know—like this," I said, rubbing my thumbs and fingers together. It was her turn to look surprised. "With your hands?" "Yeah," I said. "It's much easier that way."

And so it is. Take off any rings or jewelry and put your hands in the bowl and rub the butter and flour between your fingers. It's faster than a pastry cutter or two knives, and nearly as fast—and effective—as using a food processor. And despite all the dire warnings against warming the butter with your hands, I've never had a problem with the texture of my pastry crust.

## 8

# BREADS, SCONES, AND BUNS

## A Flour Cake

A quart of flour two eggs beat up yolks and whites two spoonfulls of barm and as much warm milk and water as will wet it, knead it well and shape it lay it before the fire to rise half an hour and bake it another half hour.

—from an 18th century Irish cookbook manuscript

If there's no bread in the house, it's as if there's no food, and any Irish cook worth his or her salt can generally whip up a batch of scones or soda bread. They're nearly the same thing, but somehow that difference in shape affects the texture. White scones or fruit scones (as they're called when you add raisins) seem dense and creamy, while white soda bread is fluffy and lighter. Both, like most Irish foods, benefit from lashings of good butter.

These breads, leavened by the chemical interaction of baking soda and buttermilk or sour milk, are what Americans call "quick breads." But for us, this is just "bread," and we distinguish between them and "yeast breads." Baking soda, in fact, is merely called "bread soda" in Ireland, so crucial is it to the bread-making process, and it's generally sold in large bags. The most important thing to know about soda breads is that they're meant to be eaten the day they're made. Scones are good warm; breads should probably cool.

Most yeast breads are bought at the store, particularly "batch," which is a dense white loaf, heavy and full of flavor, baked in large batches with the sides of each loaf butted up against the next so when the baker separates the cooled loaves, they are delicate and white while the top is firm and dark brown. Some American sources will overnight batch to you, and it's worth seeking out (p. ooo) because it makes the best toast in the world.

I wish I could buy in the United States the kind of barmbrack I love at home, but to get the good stuff, you have to make it yourself. Packaged ones are too often dry and underspiced. The recipe here makes the kind I yearn for from my childhood, with raisins and golden raisins soaked overnight in tea (and sometimes a shot of whiskey), and kneaded into a buttery, egg-rich dough, fragrant with warm spices. It's served in thick slices, thickly buttered, with a mug of milky tea, and it's the classic Halloween treat, complete with a paper-wrapped coin inside to give luck to the finder.

# WHITE SCONES

White scones are more cake-like than brown scones, and they're usually sweeter as well. They're an afternoon tea sort of treat, or the kind of thing you'd bake for a leisurely weekend breakfast, or treat yourself to in a teashop after a morning's shopping. They're so fast, however, that they could also be whipped up as an afternoon snack. Serve them split and anointed with butter, or butter and jam, or filled with strawberry jam and whipped or clotted cream. The baking powder may seem like overkill, what with the action of the baking soda and buttermilk, but it truly does help them rise high and puffy.

*Makes 1 dozen*

**3¾ cups all-purpose flour, plus more for kneading**
**½ teaspoon salt**
**¼ cup sugar**
**1 teaspoon baking powder**
**1 teaspoon baking soda**
**½ cup (1 stick) butter**
**1 egg**
**¾ cup buttermilk**
**¼ cup heavy cream**

1   Preheat the oven to 450 degrees F and lightly grease a rimless baking sheet.

2   Stir together the dry ingredients in a large bowl. Cut the butter into pieces and use your fingers to rub it into the flour, or use two knives or a fork to cut it in, until the mixture resembles coarse crumbs.

3   Beat the egg and mix with the buttermilk. Make a well in the center of the flour and add the liquid all at once. Stir just until dough is soft. Don't overmix.

4   Lightly flour a work surface and turn the dough out onto it. Pat into a square about 1-inch thick and cut them into 12 squares. (You can also cut the dough into circles with a biscuit cutter, but patting it gently and cutting it once into squares keeps the dough from being overworked and thus makes the scones more tender.)

5   Transfer to the baking sheet. If you like, brush the surface of each with the cream to give them a sheen. Bake for 12 to 14 minutes, until puffed and golden.

## Fruit Scones

Add 1 cup raisins or golden raisins to the flour mixture after cutting in the butter.

## Brown Scones

Substitute 1¾ cups stoneground wholemeal flour for 1¾ cups all-purpose flour, and reduce the sugar to 2 tablespoons. Increase the baking time by about 5 minutes.

# ROCK CAKES (DROP SCONES)

These are named—I have always trusted—for their big craggy exterior and not for their texture. They're essentially a drop scone, and the fruit in them and the firmish dough means they drop onto the baking sheet with plenty of peaks visible in the dough. They bake up with more of a crunchy exterior, but inside they're a tender fruit scone. Sprinkling them liberally with a coarse sanding sugar makes them look prettier. Because you don't have to pat them out, they're faster and easier to slap in the oven, which is perhaps why they have a slightly more down-market feel: They're delicious, but they're considered kid food. The baking powder is non-traditional, but it's there as extra insurance to help make them fluffy and light. The recipe will still work fine if you leave it out.

*Makes 1 dozen*

**4 cups all-purpose flour**
**1 teaspoon salt**
**1 teaspoon baking powder**
**1 teaspoon baking soda**
**½ cup (1 stick) butter**
**¼ cup sugar**
**1½ cups raisins or golden raisins**
**1¼ cups buttermilk**
**1 egg**
**Coarse sugar for sprinkling (optional)**

1   Preheat the oven to 425 degrees F and lightly grease a large rimless baking sheet.

2   In a large bowl, stir together the dry ingredients and cut in the butter until the mixture resembles coarse crumbs. Stir in the raisins.

3   Beat the egg with the buttermilk. Make a well in the center of the mixture and pour in the liquid all at once. Stir just to combine, don't overmix.

4   Drop 12 big scones on the baking sheet, three across, four down. Sprinkle liberally with the coarse sugar, if using. Bake for 13 to 15 minutes, until raised and golden.

# CLASSIC BROWN SODA

This is the master recipe for basic "brown soda." If you lived in Ireland at any time over the last couple of centuries, you've eaten a basic brown soda like this, possibly even one cooked over a turf fire in a bastible. (Those who know say a turf smoke gives it an indefinable but necessary flavor. I've always managed fine with the oven.) It is usually served for breakfast, accompanying the rashers, sausages, and eggs. Served with butter, it's standard issue with a bowl of lunchtime soup, and it's a sandwich with sharp Irish cheese and a tangy relish (see Onion Marmalade, p. 300). A new loaf generally appears for afternoon tea, sliced thinner and eaten simply with butter, as a matter of course, before eating cake or sweets. But that's not all. Oysters wouldn't taste the same in Ireland unless they were followed by a bite of brown bread, and suffice it to say, it would be heresy to serve smoked salmon without a fresh-cut loaf.

Don't forget to cut a cross in the top. Some say it's to let the fairies escape, but whether you're concerned about spirits in your bread or not, the cross helps the bread bake evenly, and, after it has cooled, lets you break it into four even-sized "farls" for cutting.

*Makes 1 medium loaf, 6 to 8 servings*

3 cups coarse, stoneground whole-wheat flour
1 cup all-purpose flour
1 teaspoon baking soda
1 teaspoon salt
1½ to 1¾ cups buttermilk

1  Preheat the oven to 425 degrees F.

2  In a large mixing bowl, stir together the flours, soda, and salt. Add enough of the buttermilk to make a stiff dough.

3  Sprinkle a little flour on a rimless baking sheet and turn out the dough onto the floured surface. Shape the dough into a round and use a sharp knife to slice a large X about an inch deep across the entire surface.

4  Bake for 30 to 40 minutes, until risen and golden-brown on top. The bottom should sound hollow when tapped and a tester should come out with a few crumbs clinging to it. Wrap in a clean tea towel and cool completely on a rack before slicing.

# MOIST BROWN BREAD

This is like the luxury auto version of regular brown soda's runabout car. It's got a heap of extra bran in it, sometimes an egg, and either buttermilk or yogurt. All of us home bakers trying to make this are trying to emulate McCambridge's, which has been purveying this dense and fragrantly wheaty bread since the 1930's. Their version is, fair enough, a trade secret, and if I could get McCambridge's regularly in New York, I would never bake it myself again. Until that day comes, however, this version comes pretty close. Part of the secret is the wheat bran, and part is the very wet dough, which requires a loaf pan. You don't have to use butter or an egg—the commercial brands don't contain any—but they help make a moister bread for home cooks.

Makes 1 8 × 4-inch loaf

2½ cups stoneground whole-wheat flour
½ cup all purpose flour
½ cup wheat germ
¼ cup wheat bran
1½ teaspoons salt
1½ teaspoons baking soda
¼ cup (½ stick) butter, at room temperature
1 egg
1½ cups buttermilk

1   Preheat the oven to 375 degrees F and butter an 8 × 4-inch baking pan.

2   In a large bowl, stir together the flours, germ, bran, salt, and soda. Using your fingers, rub in the butter till the mixture forms coarse crumbs.

3   Beat the egg into the buttermilk. Make a well in the center of the dry ingredients and pour in the buttermilk mixture. Stir to combine, then turn the batter into the prepared loaf pan.

4   Bake for 45 to 50 minutes, until the surface is crusty and cracked, or until a tester inserted in the center comes out with a few crumbs clinging to it.

5   Cool completely in the pan before removing.

Bread racks outside a bakery in Bantry, Co. Cork

## It's All in the Bran

Be sure to buy stoneground wheat flour for the best texture. The added wheat bran and germ will achieve the true, moist nutty, flavor of real Irish soda bread, but it also helps to use un-iodized salt for best flavor. (If using kosher salt, add an extra 1/2 teaspoon.)

Wrapping the bread in a towel to cool makes the loaf more manageable by softening the very crunchy exterior. The towel traps the steam as the bread cools and prevents the crust from getting too hard—and prevents the loaf from drying out.

Soda bread is not meant to last to a second day, but if you do have leftovers, wrap them tightly in plastic and toast slices before serving.

### THE BASTIBLE

My father had an uncle, Uncle Barney, who was a bachelor farmer all his days. He lived alone in a thatched cottage on the Ratoath road in County Meath, a place that is now practically a freeway it's so busy with commuters and the new housing developments of the boom years. But Barney was spared all that. He smoked a pipe incessantly by the time I knew him, and every other day, he baked himself a fresh cake of soda bread in his bastible. As I've mentioned, this once-indispensable implement in any Irish cottage is a large, lidded, cast-iron pot standing securely on three short legs. Barney would stand the bastible in the burning embers of his turf fire, slap the cake of bread in the bottom, put on the lid, and shovel some of the glowing chunks of turf on top of the lid. Less than an hour later, he'd draw it out of the fire and take off the lid to reveal perfectly baked bread.

# WHITE SODA BREAD

A true white soda, unlike a scone enriched with butter and sometimes egg, doesn't have much in it, and so our white soda tends to be sort of bland. Like everyone else, I nearly always prefer brown soda bread, because it's full of so much more flavor (and that's why you get it, with butter, accompanying nearly everything you order in a restaurant). White soda is more cake-like in texture. If it has raisins and a little sugar in it, it becomes a "fruit soda," and it's a little moister and more enticing.

I have noticed the soda breads made by the American-Irish are a very different product from white soda bread in Ireland. They often have caraway seeds, something you never see in Irish soda bread (although you do see them in Seedcake, p. 000) and they're enriched with all sorts of goodies, including orange zest and eggs and butter. I suspect the Irish immigrants of long ago got to this land of plenty and thought, Why are we eating this dull, plain bread? And so they began to make additions, and I say their bread is all the better for it! Here's a plain white soda, however, the classic version, and even I have to admit that buttered white soda is good with a cup of tea or a bowl of soup, and it's a nice accompaniment to a fry-up.

Makes 1 medium loaf, 6 to 8 servings
**3½ cups all-purpose flour**
**2 to 3 tablespoons sugar**
**1½ teaspoons salt**
**1 teaspoon baking soda**
**1½ to 1¾ cups buttermilk**

1   Preheat the oven to 425 degrees F.

2   In a large bowl, stir together the flour, sugar, salt, and baking soda.

3   Stir in enough buttermilk to make a stiff dough.

4   Lightly flour a rimless baking sheet and turn out the dough onto it. Shape it into a large round. Lift it onto a baking sheet and slash the surface with a sharp knife to make an X about an inch deep across the entire surface.

5   Bake for 35 to 45 minutes, until golden and crusty. A tester should have only a few crumbs clinging to it, and the bread should sound hollow when the bottom is tapped. (If it doesn't, remove it from the baking sheet and turn it upside down directly on the oven rack and bake for 5 to 10 minutes more.) Remove from the oven and wrap it in a clean tea towel and leave it, wrapped, to cool on a wire rack. (Wrapping it traps some of the escaping steam and keeps the exterior from being unpalatably hard.)

# BARMBRACK

Barmbracks fall somewhere between a cake and a bread, doughy and yeast-raised but slightly sweet and spicy and enriched with butter, sugar, and eggs—almost like an Irish brioche. If you want to do this the traditional way, wrap a shiny new coin and a (toy) ring in a bit of parchment, and bury the coin and ring inside each round of dough before you place them in the cake pans for the final rise. Whoever gets the ring in his or her slice is supposed to marry in the coming year, and whoever gets the coin will have luck, or wealth, or what have you. Just don't forget to tell your guests there's a treasure hidden inside. Irish people expect not to bite down too hard on a piece of brack before gingerly feeling it for coins, but Americans may be very surprised indeed! Soaking the fruit in tea and whiskey adds flavor and an authentic edge to this very elegant fall dessert. Colcannon (p. 153) and brack are both autumnal foods, and they are a given for supper on Halloween night. Serve the brack sliced and thickly buttered, with a mug of milky tea.

Makes 2 8-inch bracks, about 24 servings
For the fruit:

1½ cups strong brewed tea
¼ cup Irish whiskey
1½ cups raisins
½ cup golden raisins
¾ cup mixed candied peel

For the yeast:
1¼ cups whole milk
1 package double-acting active dry yeast (2 teaspoons)
1 tablespoon sugar
1½ cups all-purpose flour

For the brack:
½ cup (1 stick) butter, softened
⅓ cup light brown sugar
1 teaspoon salt
1 teaspoon Mixed Spice (see p. 196)
2 eggs
3 cups all-purpose flour

1   Put the tea and the whiskey in a medium bowl and stir in the raisins, golden raisins, and candied peel. Cover the bowl and set aside to soak for about an hour.

2   Heat the milk in a medium bowl in the microwave (or in a small saucepan on the stovetop) until it's just warm enough to hold your finger in it without getting burned, about 115 degrees F on an instant-read thermometer. (If you overheat, let it cool back down, checking it several times with the thermometer. Milk hotter than 115 degrees F will kill the yeast.) Stir in the sugar, then sprinkle the yeast over the surface, letting it sink in and dissolve. Whisk gently with a fork. It's okay if there are small lumps of yeast. Stir in the flour to make a soft dough, cover the bowl, and set aside for 30 minutes, until doubled in size.

3   When ready to mix, fit a standing mixer with a dough hook and put in the butter, sugar, mixed spice, and salt. Beat it at low speed until creamy. Beat in the eggs and then slowly add the flour to make a smooth dough. On low speed, blend in the milk and yeast mixture, and knead at medium speed for 6 to 7 minutes to make a smooth, elastic dough. (If mixing and kneading by hand, turn the dough out onto a flour surface, knead for 5 minutes, then let the dough rest for 15 minutes. Knead again for 5 minutes until the dough is smooth and elastic.)

4   Lift out the dough, put a little oil in the bottom of the bowl, and turn the dough to coat. Cover with plastic wrap and let the bowl stand in a draft-free place for 1 hour, until the dough has doubled in size. While the dough is rising, drain the fruit and peel and spread it on a double thickness of paper towels to dry for a while.

5   When the dough has doubled, turn it onto a lightly floured surface and pat it into a large rectangle. Spread the fruit over the dough and then fold it three ways, like a letter. Turn it 90 degrees, pat into a rectangle, and fold like a letter again. Repeat 2 or 3 more times, until the fruit is worked evenly through the dough. Return to the bowl, cover, and leave for half an hour.

6   Grease two 8-inch cake pans and line them with a circle of parchment or foil. Butter the parchment as well. Divide the dough in two and fold each piece like a letter one more time, pressing them down into the pans with the fold downward and the smooth "back" of the letter on top. Cover with plastic wrap and let rise for an hour.

7   Half an hour after the dough starts this final rise, preheat the oven to 400 degrees F. Bake the risen pans for 45 to 50 minutes, until puffed and golden brown. The barmbracks are finished when a tester inserted in the center emerges clean. Cool for 15 minutes in the cake pans, then turn out and cool completely, right side up, on racks. To cut, slice each brack in half across the center, then turn each half, cut side down, and slice each half into 12 pieces.

---

MIXED SPICE

In the same way most Americans have "chili powder" in their cabinets (in Ireland, chile powder is merely ground chiles, not a blend meant for chili con carne), most Irish people have a container of "mixed spice" in theirs. It's a blend of warm spices and it's used so often in baking that most Irish recipes, such as for Christmas cake or pudding, merely call for such-and-such amount "mixed spice." It's kind of like Apple Pie Spice, but the blend is different, with a dominant scent of nutmeg and cloves. Here's how to make your own blend of mixed spice, to have on hand for baking:

Makes 2 tablespoons
1 tablespoon ground cinnamon
2 teaspoons freshly grated nutmeg
1 teaspoon ground cloves
1 teaspoon ground allspice

Blend in a small jar and store tightly closed.

# HOT CROSS BUNS

Easter is a big deal in Ireland and I like the way the holiday is used to mark time. "Please God, you'll be back with us at Easter," a parent might say to a visiting adult child at Christmas. By Easter, it is deep into spring and the country is in full bloom. Lambs are bouncing about the countryside, tulips are bursting forth, and cherry trees are in blossom. No wonder we take our hot cross buns so seriously and eat them throughout the season! They are part of the package that says life has returned and it'll be summer before long.

Makes 1 dozen
1 cup whole milk
½ cup (1 stick) butter
½ cup sugar
1 package active dry yeast (2 teaspoons)
4 cups all-purpose flour
2 teaspoons Mixed Spice (p. [ooo])
¼ teaspoon salt
2 eggs
1 cup fresh, soft raisins (if yours are old and dry, buy a new box)
¼ cup candied peel, chopped

For the glaze:
1 egg
1 tablespoon water
For the cross:
½ cup all-purpose flour
¼ cup water
2 tablespoons confectioners' sugar
1 tablespoon butter, melted

1   Heat the milk and butter in the microwave or on the stovetop just until the butter melts and the milk is hand-hot—so it feels hot but doesn't burn your finger to dip it in the milk. Check with an instant-read thermometer that it's no hotter than 115 degrees F; if so, let it cool because hotter milk will kill the yeast. Stir the sugar into the milk, sprinkle the yeast over all, and whisk with a fork to dissolve the yeast. Allow to sit for 10 minutes until foamy.

2   While the yeast foams, put the flour, mixed spice, and salt in a stand mixer fitted with a dough hook. With the mixer on low, slowly pour in the yeast and milk mixture. Add the eggs one at a time, mixing until combined. Add the raisins and mixed peel, stirring to combine.

3   With the mixer on medium, knead for 4 to 5, minutes until the dough is smooth and shiny, and the fruit is distributed throughout the dough. Lift the dough out of the mixer bowl, pour a little oil in the bottom, and turn the dough to coat in the oil. Cover with plastic wrap and set aside in a draft-free place to rise until doubled in size.

4   On a lightly floured surface, divide the dough into 12 even balls. Turn each ball inside out, leaving the stretched part as the new exterior and pinching the bottoms together like a balloon. Set the pinched side down on a large rimless baking sheet. Continue with all the dough. Cover loosely with a large sheet of plastic wrap and set aside in a draft-free place to rise until doubled in size, about 30 minutes.

5   Preheat the oven to 400 degrees F. Beat the egg with 1 tablespoon water to make a glaze. In a small bowl, whisk together the flour, water, confectioners' sugar, and melted butter. Brush the egg glaze on the raised buns. If you don't have a piping bag with a plain tip, put the flour and water mixture into a ziplock bag, seal it, and cut a tiny tip off one bottom corner. (Make a small cut first; you can always enlarge it.) Pipe a generous cross about 1/2-inch wide over the entire top of each bun, dividing each bun into four quarters.

6   Bake for 15 to 17 minutes, until puffed and golden. Cool on a rack until barely warm.

# OLD-FASHIONED SPICY GINGERBREAD

Much gingerbread is so mild-flavored and neutral that there may as well not be any ginger in it. This recipe calls for a generous two tablespoons which makes gingerbread with a real spicy kick to it. There's so much warm spice in this recipe—cloves, cinnamon, cardamom—this is one recipe that will in fact taste much better the next day when the gingerbread is cool and the flavors have had time to meld and bloom. I like to bake it in a loaf pan and serve it cut into thick, moist slices. Try sandwiching two slices with a little cream cheese and thinly sliced tart apple for an unconventional but excellent lunch. You can also bake it in a buttered 9 × 9-inch pan; just reduce the baking time to 20 to 25 minutes.

*Makes 6 to 8 servings*
1½ cups flour
½ teaspoon baking soda
2 tablespoons ground ginger
1 teaspoon ground cinnamon
¼ teaspoon ground cloves
¼ teaspoon ground cardamom
½ teaspoon salt
½ cup (1 stick) unsalted butter, softened
½ cup dark brown sugar
1 cup molasses
2 eggs
½ cup buttermilk

1   Preheat the oven to 350 degrees F and lightly butter a 9-inch loaf tin. Put the dry ingredients in a medium bowl and whisk to combine.

2   Cream the butter and sugar until fluffy using an electric mixer, then add the eggs and molasses. Mix to combine, then stir in the buttermilk. The mixture will appear loose and not emulsified. That's okay.

3   Add the dry ingredients and stir until no flour streaks show. Turn the batter into the prepared pan and bake 40 to 50 minutes, until a tester inserted in the center comes out with a few crumbs clinging to it. Cool in the pan for 15 minutes, then remove the gingerbread from the pan and cool completely on a wire rack.

# OATCAKES

On first glance, these plain little cakes might seem to be so ordinary they're hardly worth bothering with. But their utter simplicity—the mild oat flavor and the nubbly texture of the rolled oats—is what makes them so addictively good with cheese. I like them best of all with a high-quality sharp cheddar, the kind with the classic fudgy, crumbly texture, but they're an ideal cheese biscuit, ready to accompany whatever cheese you're eating. You can buy readymade oatcakes good and bad at any Irish supermarket, but the freshness and crunch of the home-baked version is unparalleled.

*Makes 4 servings*

¼ cup water

2 tablespoons butter

1 cup old-fashioned rolled oats (not quick oats), plus more for rolling

¼ cup all-purpose flour

¼ teaspoon salt

¼ teaspoon baking soda

1   Preheat the oven to 350 degrees F and lightly grease a rimless baking sheet. Put the water and butter in a small saucepan (or in a bowl in the microwave) and heat just until the butter melts completely. Remove from the heat.

2   Stir together the oats, flour, salt, and soda into a medium bowl. Stir in the water and butter to make a stiff dough.

3   Scatter additional oatmeal on a clean work surface and turn the dough out onto it. Knead lightly one or two times, then divide the dough in two. Scattering more oatmeal as needed to prevent sticking, pat each piece into a circle 1/4-inch thick. Cut each circle into four quarters, and use a spatula to lift them onto the prepared baking sheet.

4   Bake for 20 to 25 minutes, until the oatcakes are just turning golden around the edges but are not browned. Cool on a rack before serving.

## 9

# CAKES AND TEA THINGS

## Very Good Lemon Cake

Take a pound of sugar pound and sift it three quarters pound of the choicest flour 12 eggs but only six whites grate the rind of two large lemons beet the eggs with a whisk until they are light and thick, then put in your sugar by degrees and put it in your flour after the same manner, mix the lemon peel with two or three spoonfulls of batter then put it to the rest and continue beating of it till the oven be ready put in a tin pan floured then set it in a quick oven an hour will bake it, if you please you may put in some sweet meats.

—from an 18<sup>th</sup> century Irish cookbook manuscript

Ireland is a great land of cakes. We're not so big on little fiddly sweets, and we like our biscuits (which is what we call cookies as well as crackers) pretty straightforward, but we have a huge variety of cakes, and many of them involve dried fruit, which makes them moist and sweet. An old-fashioned Victorian afternoon tea involved bread and butter, followed by a slice of cake, and that cake came from what used to be known as "cutting cakes," meant to be well-wrapped and stored for repeated tastes.

This discrete—and frankly, discreet—enjoyment of sweets is very Irish. It would be frowned upon to fall upon a cake and eat it all at one sitting—even by a large group. You always have to leave a bit behind to show you're not being greedy. When visiting friends, it was always an accepted part of Irish social discourse for the guest not to accept a cup of tea and something to eat until the third offer. If offered thrice, the host truly meant it, and the visitor had demurred enough and could now accept.

Even today (when you might safely say yes to the first offer of a cuppa!), it's comforting to know there's a mild-flavored cutting cake not far away, perhaps an everyday sort of fruitcake, sometimes called an Oxford Lunch, ready for a quick nibble, or a caraway-scented Seedcake (we do eat caraway in cake, just not in soda bread), or a pleasantly biting Ginger Cake, made with copious amounts of candied ginger in syrup. What is not for us, most of the time, is the glorious layer cake with fancy icings. We tend to like our sweets a bit more understated. Perhaps we do have a national sweet tooth after all! Why else would we need all this cake permanently on hand?

# SEEDCAKE

I always associate Seedcake with my mother's hometown of Ballina, in County Mayo, where my mother's Auntie Martina would have one wrapped up in the pantry, doling out a slice now and then with a wink. It's a rich pound cake with so much caraway in it the first slice will make you blink. Once you surrender to the overwhelming note of caraway, however, it's soothing and aromatic, a memorable taste in the buttery crumb of the cake. Seedcake is so potent it's meant to be cut in small slices, about ½-inch thick.

*Makes 12 servings*
¾ cup (1½ sticks) butter
1 cup sugar
3 eggs
2 cups all-purpose flour
½ teaspoon baking powder
1½ tablespoons caraway seeds

1   Preheat the oven to 350 degrees F and butter an 8 × 4-inch loaf pan. Line it with parchment paper.

2   With a hand mixer, cream the butter and sugar together in a medium mixing bowl until very light in color. Beat in the eggs, continuing to mix for 3 to 4 minutes, until pale and fluffy.

3   Mix in the flour and baking powder. Add the caraway seeds, saving out about half a teaspoon. Turn the mixture into the prepared loaf pan and smooth cake batter along the length of the pan. Sprinkle the top with the reserved caraway.

4   Bake for 35 to 40 minutes, until golden brown. Cool for 5 minutes in the pan, then turn out of the pan and cool right side up on a wire rack. Store wrapped in parchment paper, and then sealed into a ziplock bag with all the air pushed out. Kept tightly wrapped, it's good for up to two weeks.

# EVERYDAY FRUITCAKE

Candied fruit and candied peel are regulars on the baking shelves in Irish supermarkets, not just something that appears at Christmas time. That's because a lot of our baking contains candied fruit or cherries or mixed peel. We like the sort of astringent flavors they offer, a nice contrast against the sweetness of butter and sugar. This simple fruitcake is a good example. It's also called Oxford Lunch, and you can buy versions in any Irish supermarket under that name, but I tend to think of it as "Everyday Fruitcake," for that is what it is.

Makes 18 servings

½ cup (1 stick) butter
1 cup sugar
3 eggs
¼ cup ground almonds
Juice and zest of 1 orange
2½ cups all-purpose flour
½ teaspoon baking powder
1 cup raisins
1 cup golden raisins
½ cup candied cherries

1   Preheat the oven to 300 degrees F and butter a 9 × 5-inch loaf tin. Line the bottom with parchment.

2   In a mixing bowl, using a hand mixer, beat together the butter and sugar until fluffy. Add the eggs, one at a time, beating well after each. Blend in the ground almonds, orange zest, and juice.

3   Stir in the flour and baking powder just to combine. Stir in the raisins, golden raisins, and cherries. Turn the batter into the prepared pan and smooth the top.

4   Bake for 2 hours. It's a long and slow cooking time because the heavy batter is so freighted with fruit. If a tester comes out clean after 2 hours, you're done, but you may need as long as 30 minutes more, depending on the moistness of your fruit. Cool in the pan for 30 minutes, then carefully remove to a cooling rack, right side up, and cool completely before cutting.

# PORTER CAKE

On the one hand, this cake is nothing more than a sort of everyday fruitcake that's dark; on the other hand, it's so much more: the addition of porter (there *are* other porters and stouts besides Guinness, but I don't use them) brings depth and complexity to the finished product, brightened by orange zest and speckled with candied cherries. Wrapped well and sealed in an airtight container, this is an ideal "cutting cake" that will keep well for a week or ten days, perfect to serve at an afternoon tea.

*Makes 24 servings*

4 cups all-purpose flour

1½ teaspoons baking soda

½ teaspoon salt

2 teaspoons Mixed Spice (p. 196)

1 cup (2 sticks) butter

1 cup sugar

2 eggs

Zest of one orange

1 12-ounce bottle Guinness

1 cup golden raisins

1 cup raisins

½ cup mixed candied peel

1   Preheat the oven to 350 degrees F. Butter a 9-inch cake pan and line it with parchment paper. Sift together the flour, baking soda, salt, and mixed spice into a medium bowl.

2   Using a mixer, in a large bowl cream the butter and sugar until fluffy. Beat in the eggs, one at a time, and the orange zest. With the mixer on low speed, add half the flour, then half the Guinness, followed by the remaining flour and Guinness and mixing well after each addition.

3   Stir in the raisins, golden raisins, and mixed candied peel. Turn the mixture into the prepared cake pan and bake for 1 ½ hours, until a tester in the center comes out clean. Cool completely on a rack in the pan before cutting.

# DUNDEE CAKE

My granny was famous for her Dundee Cake, a rich golden cake discreetly studded with glace cherries, swelling regally under its spiraling decorative paving of whole blanched almonds. My Aunt Mary, Granny's youngest daughter, inherited her mother's baking genes, and every year she graciously makes a Christmas Pudding and a Dundee Cake for my family. Mary's pudding is always excellent, but we can't wait to cut her Dundee Cake, so dense and rich and full of flavor, temptingly wrapped in greaseproof paper and tied up with twine. We try to hold out until St. Stephen's Day before we attack it, but I confess everyone: Last year I'm the one who cut the twine on Christmas night and had a little nibble. I also confess this recipe isn't nearly as good as my Aunt Mary's, but she's the holder of that family secret, so this will have to do.

*Makes 24 servings*

**2 cups blanched whole almonds**

**2 cups currants**

**1 cup raisins**

**1 cup golden raisins**

**⅔ cup candied peel**

**⅔ cup glace cherries**

**Zest of 1 lemon**

**¼ cup sherry or brandy**

**3 cups all-purpose flour**

**1½ teaspoons Mixed Spice (p. 211)**

**½ teaspoon salt**

**1 cup (2 sticks) butter**

**1½ cups sugar**

**½ cup light brown sugar**

**4 eggs**

1  Preheat the oven to 300 degrees F and butter a 3-inch deep, 9-inch diameter cake tin. Line the sides and bottom with a double thickness of parchment paper. (Cut two circles for the base and two long strips for the sides, buttering them to help them stick. This layering helps prevent the cake from getting too dark during the long cooking time.)

2  In a medium bowl, mix 1 cup of the almonds, all the fruit, the candied peel, cherries, lemon zest, and sherry or brandy. Sift the flour, mixed spice, and salt onto a sheet of waxed paper.

3  In a large mixing bowl, beat the butter, sugar, and brown sugar until creamy. Don't overbeat to make it fluffy. Add the eggs, one at a time, beating just to combine. Stir in the flour and spice, and then add the fruit mixture. Stir to completely combine but don't over mix. You don't want to add air here.

4  Turn the cake into the prepared pan, and cover the top with the remaining almonds, turning them pointed side inward in a swirling rosette pattern. Bake for 2 ½ to 3 hours, until a tester in the center comes out clean.

# CHOCOLATE GUINNESS CAKE

When you add Guinness to chocolate desserts, people often can't identify it, but the two pair beautifully. Buried in the depths of a freshly pulled Guinness in a proper Irish pint glass (20 ounces, not 16!), you can taste hints of chocolate. And when the Guinness is buried in a moist chocolate cake, you can taste hints of Guinness's creamy and appealing bitterness. This cake is surprisingly child-friendly—the alcohol cooks off entirely, and it is chocolate cake, after all—but adults will appreciate the depth and complexity of flavors in it. You can use all-purpose flour here, but cake flour helps ensure a velvety crumb. Melting the butter instead of creaming it makes a dense and moist cake that's easy to throw together.

*Makes 12 servings*

**1 12-ounce bottle Guinness Extra Stout**

**½ cup (1 stick) butter**

**2 cups sugar**

**½ cup unsweetened cocoa powder**

**½ cup sour cream**

**2 eggs**

**2 teaspoons vanilla**

**2 cups cake flour**

**1 teaspoon baking soda**

**½ teaspoon baking powder**

1 Preheat the oven to 350 degrees F and butter a 9-inch round cake pan. Butter the bottom and line it with parchment paper.

2 In a large saucepan over medium heat, heat the Guinness and butter just until the butter melts. Whisk in the sugar and cocoa.

3 With the batter still in the large saucepan, whisk in the sour cream followed by the eggs and vanilla. Beat until the mixture is smooth. Whisk in the flour, baking soda, and baking powder.

4 Turn the mixture into the prepared pan, and bake 50 to 60 minutes, until a tester in the center comes out clean. Cool 10 minutes in the pan, then turn out carefully and cool, right side up, on a cooling rack. Do not cut the cake until completely cooled.

# GUR CAKE

When I asked a friend in Dublin recently if he knew any bakery in Dublin still selling gur cake, and mentioned fondly a bakery that used to sell a good version, he laughed and said, "You are so living in a Dublin of twenty years ago!" So maybe gur cake isn't as common as it once was, but anyone in Dublin can tell you all about it (assuming they are over twenty years of age, of course). Gur cake looks like a fruit slice, which is a sort of sweet, raisin-filled pastry you'll still see in bakeries, but unlike fruit slice, the filling is primarily leftover cake—fruit cake, barmbrack, sponge cake, or even bread. Bakeries used to crumble up leftovers, mix with fruit and sugar, and encase this sweet mass between two slabs of pastry. A big slab of gur cake was a filling and cheap treat for a kid with a few pennies to spare, and it tasted different each time depending on what crumbs they used—it was all part of the charm. Gur cake made with leftover Christmas cakes and puddings was a particular favorite.

*Makes 12 servings*

1 cup strong-brewed tea
1 cup raisins
2 cups all-purpose flour
1 tablespoon sugar
¼ teaspoon salt
½ cup (1 stick) butter
⅓ to ½ cup cold water
3 cups cake crumbs (pound cake, sponge cake, chocolate cake—whatever you have)
½ cup light brown sugar
2 teaspoons Mixed Spice (p. 196)
2 tablespoons heavy cream
Coarse sanding sugar

1   The night before you begin, pour the tea in a small bowl and add the raisins. Cover and leave to soak overnight.

2   Make the pastry: In a food processor, pulse the flour, sugar, and salt. Cut the butter into 8 pieces and drop it into the machine. Pulse until the mixture forms coarse crumbs. With the machine running, start to slowly pour the cold water into food processor. As soon as the dough gathers into a ball, stop adding water. You may not need the entire half-cup.

3   Divide the pastry into two balls and wrap each in plastic wrap, flattening into a disk. Chill while you prepare the filling.

4   Put the cake crumbs in a large mixing bowl and pour the tea and raisins over all. Stir with a wooden spoon to break up any cake chunks. Add the sugar and mixed spice. Taste and add a little more mixed spice if you prefer.

5   Preheat the oven to 400 degrees F and butter a 7 by 11-inch baking dish. On a lightly floured surface, roll one disk of pastry to a rectangle and fit it into the baking dish. It's okay if it runs up the sides a bit.

6   Spoon the cake filling into the pastry in the pan, and roll out the second disk of pastry to a rectangle. Cover the filling completely, trimming off the excess, and use the tip of a sharp paring knife to slash several vents in the surface of the pastry. Brush the surface with the heavy cream and, if you like, sprinkle with the sanding sugar.

7   Bake for 30 to 35 minutes, until the pastry is golden brown. Cool completely before cutting. Slice the gur cake into 12 rectangles.

# LIGHT AND MOIST CANDIED GINGER CAKE

This is not a dark and spicy gingerbread, but instead a pale gold cake containing the sweet bite of candied ginger. If you can't find candied stem ginger in syrup, look for plain dry candied ginger, the kind rolled in a little sugar, and use a cupful of it, chopped. Be sure not to over bake because this is not a cake you want to dry out. Once a tester shows a few crumbs clinging to it, take the cake out of the oven and let it cool.

*Makes 1 8-inch round*
½ cup (1 stick) butter, softened
¾ cup dark brown sugar
3 eggs
1½ cups all-purpose flour
1 teaspoon baking soda
1 teaspoon ground ginger
½ cup buttermilk
1 cup chopped stem ginger in syrup, chopped into a medium dice

1   Preheat the oven to 350 degrees F and butter an 8-inch cake pan.

2   With a mixer, beat the butter and sugar until fluffy. Beat in the eggs, one at a time, until fully combined. Sift the flour, baking soda, and ground ginger directly into the bowl and mix just to combine. Pour in the buttermilk and mix on low until no streaks of flour remain.

3   Stir in the chopped ginger and turn the batter into the pan. Bake for 25 to 30 minutes, until the surface is lightly golden and a tester in the center comes out with a few crumbs clinging to it. Cool completely before cutting.

# IRISH BATTENBURG CAKE

This checkered cake was invented during the Victorian era to celebrate the wedding of one of Queen Victoria's granddaughters to a German prince—not exactly an auspicious start for a cake widely enjoyed in Ireland. But the two countries share more than a climate: they also have a liking for tasty treats to accompany an afternoon cup of tea. I've updated the pink and white of the traditional Battenburg cake to a green and white check and wrapped it not in plain white marzipan but in marzipan of an orange hue to make the whole thing decidedly Irish. It looks like a million bucks when you're done, and it's a lot easier to make than it looks.

Makes 8 to 10 servings

½ cup (1 stick) butter, softened

½ cup sugar

2 eggs

2 tablespoons milk

½ teaspoon vanilla

1½ cups all-purpose flour

½ teaspoon baking powder

Pinch of salt

Green food coloring

Confectioners' sugar for sprinkling

1 7-ounce tube marzipan

Red and yellow food coloring

¼ cup apricot jam

1 Preheat the oven to 350 degrees F and grease two 8 × 4-inch loaf pans.

2 Beat the butter and sugar with a mixer until fluffy, then add the eggs, milk, and vanilla, beating to combine. Sift the flour, baking powder, and salt directly into the bowl, and mix just until no streaks remain.

3 Spoon half the batter into one of the prepared pans, leveling it out to the sides so the cake bakes evenly and doesn't dome in the center. Stir three drops of green food coloring into the remaining batter in the bowl, then spoon the green batter into the other pan and level it. Bake both pans for 12 to 15 minutes, until a tester in the center comes out clean. Cool for 10 minutes in the pans, then turn onto a rack and cool completely.

4 While the cakes are baking, line a clean work surface with a large square of parchment paper or wax paper. Dust with confectioners' sugar and put the marzipan on the parchment. Knead it with your hands until pliable, then add one drop red and one drop yellow food coloring to the surface of the marzipan. (You may want to wear rubber gloves to keep from staining your fingers.) Knead to distribute the color throughout. If you want a darker orange, add colors one drop at a time to avoid overwetting the marzipan. Set the orange marzipan aside.

5 To assemble, cut each cake in half lengthwise and brush all the exterior surfaces with apricot jam. Lay one white and one green slice side by side, pressed together, then top those two with one green and one white slice, to make a checkerboard. Press the four pieces together firmly with your hands. Sprinkle more confectioners' sugar on a clean work surface and use a rolling pin to roll the marzipan to a rectangle about 1/8-inch thick. Set the cake on the marzipan and roll it up in the marzipan, leaving the ends uncovered. Pinch the seam to seal and trim a very thin slice off each end with a serrated knife to even up the cake. Cut into 8 or 10 slices to serve.

# COFFEE CAKE

My American wife and I had our first (but certainly not the last) cultural miscommunication over coffee cake. To me, Irish it's an iced cake, coffee-flavored. To her, it was a homey, homemade morning cake to be eaten with a soothing cup of coffee. During a bout of homesickness when she was a student in Dublin, she expressed a longing for coffee cake. The next day, I brought her a cardboard bakery box. She opened it with great anticipation to find a round layer cake glistening with shiny brown icing. "What's this?" she asked. "Coffee cake," I said. "It is not." "It sure is. Taste it. Here, I'll make you a cup of tea to go with it." She couldn't hide her disappointment (I guess she really was homesick). But after she tasted it, she had to admit Irish coffee cake, a coffee-flavored sponge with coffee buttercream, was pretty good. Nowadays, she likes it with coffee. I still prefer my coffee cake, Irish-style, with tea.

*Makes 12 servings*
**1 cup (2 sticks) butter, softened**

**1 cup brown sugar**

**4 eggs**

**2 cups all-purpose flour**

**1 teaspoon baking powder**

**¼ teaspoon salt**

**1 cup milk**

**1 tablespoon instant coffee or instant espresso**

*For the icing:*
**½ cup (1 stick) butter, softened**

**1 teaspoon instant coffee, dissolved in 2 tablespoons warm milk**

**1 teaspoon vanilla**

**4 cups (about 1 pound) confectioners' sugar**

1 Preheat oven to 350 degrees F and grease and flour 2 × 9-inch round cake pans. In a mixer, cream the butter and sugar until light. Add the eggs, one at a time, beating well each time until the mixture is pale and fluffy.

2 Sift together the flour, baking powder, and salt. Heat the milk on the stovetop or in the microwave and stir in the coffee granules, until completely dissolved.

3 With the mixer running on low, add about ⅓ of the flour mixture, beating until combined, then ⅓ of the milk, continuing until all ingredients are used. Pour the batter into the prepared cake pans and smooth the surface with the back of a spoon. Bake for approximately 30 minutes, until a skewer comes out with a few crumbs clinging to it.

4 Allow the cakes to cool in the pan for 5 minutes, then turn out onto a wire rack.

5 While the cakes cool, make the icing. Beat together the butter and milk, then slowly add the confectioners' sugar until the icing is smooth, creamy, and spreadable.

6 Spread a portion of the icing on top of one cake layer as a filling, then top with the other layer and ice the sides and top of the cake with the remaining icing.

# IRISH PANCAKES

Why are pancakes in the "cakes" chapter? Well, even though they may seem to you like a breakfast food, in Ireland they're a dessert. We don't eat stacks of American pancakes with maple syrup (much as I like them now). Instead, our pancakes are very thin, crepes really, and we eat them sprinkled with lemon juice and sugar and rolled, particularly on "Pancake Tuesday," as we call Mardi Gras. Be sure you have a well-seasoned pan or a nonstick skillet for best results. Lemon juice and sugar is a favorite filling, but you can also roll them with jam or—my kids' favorite—Nutella.

*Makes 4 servings*
1 cup whole milk
2 eggs
2 tablespoons melted butter, plus more for cooking
¼ teaspoon salt
1 cup all-purpose flour

1   Put all the ingredients in a blender in the order listed and process until smooth, less than a minute. Let the batter stand for half an hour.

2   When ready to cook, heat a well-seasoned medium skillet over medium heat. Melt a little butter in the skillet and swirl it around. Then with a wadded-up paper towel, distribute the butter and soak up the excess (be careful not to burn yourself).

3   Pour about 3 tablespoons batter into the skillet and use the handle to swirl the batter to coat the pan. Let it cook for about 1 minute, then use a fork to loosen the pancake on one edge, and peel it off in one piece. Flip and lightly brown on the other side, about 30 seconds.

4   Move the pancake to a plate and keep warm while you keep cooking. At our house, on Pancake Tuesday, everyone gathers around the stove, and we eat them hot as soon as they come out of the skillet.

# DIGESTIVE BISCUITS

The kind of digestives I can't stop eating are the sugary biscuits that have oatmeal in them—and chocolate outside. But I know that super-sweet chocolate-coated digestives aren't what was originally intended by a lightly sweetened wholemeal biscuit meant to give you a little extra fiber at the end of a meal. These biscuits are a more traditional digestive, mildly sweet, wholegrain. They're actually delicious, plain, or spread with Strawberry Jam (p. 294), Lemon Curd (p. 298), or even peanut butter. Use the coarsest stoneground flour you can get. If you use traditional rolled oats, you'll get a slightly chewier cookie; quick-cooking oat flakes will disappear more into the dough. Both are good. If you happen to melt a cup of some semisweet chocolate chips and dip each finished cookie in it, I can't stop you.

Makes 2½ dozen
**1 cup stoneground whole-wheat flour**
**1 cup all-purpose flour**
**½ cup (1 stick) butter**
**1 cup rolled oats**
**½ cup light brown sugar**
**½ teaspoon salt**
**½ teaspoon baking powder**
**1 egg**
**2 tablespoons milk**

1   Preheat the oven to 400 degrees F and grease a baking sheet.

2   Put the flours in a large mixing bowl. Use a fork, two knives, or your hands to cut or rub the butter into the flour until it looks like coarse crumbs. Stir in the oatmeal, sugar, salt, and baking soda.

3   Beat the egg with the milk and pour into the flour mixture, stirring to make a stiff dough. On a lightly floured work surface, roll out half the dough and cut in 2-inch rounds. Prick each biscuit all over with a fork. Bake for 10 to 12 minutes, until lightly browned and just set. Repeat with remaining dough.

# SHORTBREAD

"Real" shortbread is typically made with a little rice flour, which gives it that dry and delicate crunch. Instead of seeking rice flour, you can get an excellent result by using cornstarch to help achieve the classic texture. Sprinkle on a little green sanding sugar to celebrate "the day that's in it," as the Irish say.

*Makes 1 8-inch round*

½ cup (1 stick) butter, softened

¾ cup flour

¼ cup cornstarch

¼ cup sugar

Pinch salt

½ teaspoon vanilla

Green sanding or decorating sugar

1   Preheat the oven to 325 degrees F and lightly grease an 8-inch round cake tin.

2   Put the butter in a medium bowl and use a hand mixer to beat until smooth. Add the remaining ingredients and mix to combine. Press into the bottom of the prepared pan, smoothing the surface with your fingertips, and chill for 10 minutes in the refrigerator.

3   Sprinkle generously with the green sugar and bake for 15 minutes, until just turning golden brown. While still warm, cut into 16 wedges with the tip of a paring knife. Let cool completely before removing from pan.

RAISING THE LID ON SELF-RISING FLOUR
The Irish often use self-rising flour for baking, although it's much less common in the US. If you're following a recipe from an Irish book or site that calls for self-rising flour, many American substitution charts will tell you to substitute 1 cup all-purpose flour plus 1 teaspoon baking powder. Do not do this! It's far too much baking powder and you'll end up with a cake or biscuits that taste like salty aluminum. A far better proportion is 1 teaspoon baking powder for every 2 cups of all-purpose flour.

# CHRISTMAS CAKE

My family tends to have a Dundee cake (p. 211) as our Christmas cake, but here's the more usual item. This dark and elaborate fruitcake is supposed to be made weeks before the holiday and "fed" brandy or whiskey every week. If you can keep up with the demands of feeding a cake, you're rewarded with complex flavors like a fine, aged wine. It's meant to be finished off with a layer of marzipan, then sealed with a glossy finish of hard royal icing, and, in the days after the holiday, savored in small slices.

*Makes about 24 servings*
**2 cups golden raisins**
**1 cup dark raisins**
**1 cup currants**
**1 cup candied cherries, halved**
**½ cup candied peel, chopped**
**2 teaspoons Mixed Spice (p. 196)**
**1 teaspoon vanilla**
**Grated zest and juice of 1 lemon**
**Grated zest and juice of 1 orange**
**¼ cup whiskey, plus more for drizzling**
**1 cup (2 sticks) butter, softened**
**1 cup light brown sugar**
**4 eggs**
**1 cup ground almonds**
**2 cups all-purpose flour**
**1 teaspoon baking powder**
**½ teaspoon salt**
**Confectioners' sugar (optional)**
**1 tube (7 ounces) marzipan (optional)**
**Royal Icing (optional, see sidebar)**

1   In a large bowl, combine all the dried fruit with the spices, vanilla, and the zest and juice of the orange and lemon. Stir in the whiskey. Cover the mixture with a plate and leave it to soak overnight.

**THE ROYAL FINISH**
Royal icing is the classic finish for Christmas Cake. It dries to a hard, glossy finish, keeping the marzipan layer beneath it moist and preventing the cake from drying out. It's easy to make, but once you've made it, use it quickly, and press plastic wrap directly over the surface from the moment you lift out the mixer to the moment you frost the cake.

To make enough royal icing for a Christmas cake, with an electric mixer, whip two egg whites with two teaspoons lemon juice until frothy. With the mixer on medium, beat in three cups of confectioners' sugar a little at a time, until the mixture is thick but still liquid enough to beat. Turn the mixer to high and continue to beat until the mixture is thick and glossy, about 3 minutes.

2   The next day, when you're ready to bake, preheat the oven to 300 degrees F. Butter the bottom of a large, deep (6-inch) cake tin, and line it with a circle of parchment, buttering the top of the paper, too.

3   In a large bowl, cream the butter and sugar until fluffy with an electric mixer. Add the eggs one at a time, beating well after each, then beat in the ground almonds.

4   Using a large wooden spoon (not the mixer), stir in the flour, baking powder, and salt. Add the fruit and all the liquid in the bowl and stir to combine. Turn the batter into the prepared pan and smooth the top. It will be quite thick.

5   Cover the pan with a layer of parchment paper and seal it with foil. This will keep the cake from burning during the long cooking time. Bake it for 3 hours, then lift off the foil and insert a skewer to test it. If the center is still wet, cover it again with the parchment and foil and bake for another 30 to 60 minutes, or until the skewer comes out clean. Let the cake cool overnight still in the cake pan.

6   The next day, gently run a knife around the outside edge and carefully turn the cake out of the pan. Poke holes all over the bottom with a skewer and drizzle a few tablespoons of whiskey into it. Wrap the whole cake in parchment paper and then foil. Keep it in the back of the refrigerator, adding a little more whiskey every week until Christmas (you can keep this up for 2 months, or you can make the cake and just age it for a few days).

7   If you don't want to frost the cake, you can serve it as is, or you can give it a heavy dusting of confectioners' sugar. To frost the cake, at least 2 days before you plan to eat it, knead the marzipan with your hands to soften it. Sprinkle a clean work surface thickly with confectioners' sugar and roll the marzipan out into a large circle. Roll it loosely around the rolling pin and lift it onto the cake, opening it over the top and sides and folding and molding it with your hands to fit it all around the cake.

8   Make the royal icing and spread it thickly over the marzipan. Leave it to dry, uncovered, for a couple of days. The icing makes an airtight seal that lets the marzipan sort of melt into the sides of the cake. It's usual to top the cake with silly Christmas figures, such as a little plastic Santa and a sleigh, or some tiny green Christmas trees and a few reindeer.

9   To serve, cut off a quarter of the cake and slice that into "fingers" about 1-inch thick. Wrap the cake tightly in plastic after cutting it.

# CHERRY CAKE

When I began making this cake from a newspaper clipping one holiday season, I'd never before heard the phrase "gluten-free." But now I realize this cake actually is, since the basis of it is eggs and ground almonds. Prior to the new wave of gluten-free products, it used to be harder to find ground almonds in the States, and I used to grind blanched whole almonds in the food processor until they were like fine cornmeal. Now you can buy almond flour in nearly any supermarket, making this delicately flavored, vaguely pink cake a breeze.

*Makes 8 servings*

**½ cup raisins**
**2 tablespoons sweet sherry**
**⅓ cup (⅔ stick) butter**
**½ cup sugar**
**3 eggs, separated**
**½ teaspoon almond extract**
**½ cup glace cherries, quartered**
**1¼ cups ground almonds**

1   Preheat the oven to 325 degrees F. Grease an 8 × 4-inch loaf pan and line the bottom with parchment or wax paper.

2   Place the raisins and sherry in a small saucepan and heat gently for 5 minutes so the raisins will absorb the sherry. Remove from the heat and stir in the cherries and 3 tablespoons of the ground almonds. Set aside.

3   In a separate bowl, cream the butter and sugar until fluffy. Beat in the egg yolks and almond extract, and stir in the remaining ground almonds. Fold in the raisins and cherries.

4   Beat the egg whites until they form stiff peaks and fold gently into the cherry batter with a large metal spoon.

5   Pour into the prepared pan and bake for about 1 hour, or until a skewer inserted in the middle comes out clean. Cool in the loaf pan. If desired, turn the cooled cake over, poke a few holes in the bottom, and drizzle it with a few tablespoons of sweet sherry. Store in an airtight container for up to 2 weeks.

## Raising the Lid on Self-Rising Flour

The Irish often use self-rising flour for baking, although it's much less common in the US. If you're following a recipe from an Irish book or site that calls for self-rising flour, many American substitution charts will tell you to substitute 1 cup all-purpose flour plus 1 teaspoon baking powder. Do not do this! It's far too much baking powder and you'll end up with a cake or biscuits that taste like salty aluminum. A far better proportion is 1 teaspoon baking powder for every 2 cups of all-purpose flour.

# DESSERTS, TARTS, PUDDINGS, AND SWEETS

## 10

## A Common Fancy

Take the crumbs of a penny loaf grated and a pint of cream ten eggs half the whites, green it with the juice of spinage, and shred a little tansy grass in, then boil it to a hasty pudding, put in two spoonsfulls of orange flower water, sugar and nutmeg to your taste then fry it.

—from an 18th century Irish cookbook manuscript

Beyond all those cakes on the tea table, we do eat desserts in Ireland. Apples are a running theme, but we use them, like potatoes, in a lot of different ways—from the Potato-Apple Cake, a recipe that dates back several hundred years, to the soft fluffiness of the pudding called Apple Snow, to sharply sweet Irish Apple Tarts, not drowned with cinnamon but spiced only with cloves.

There's also a lot of whipped cream, for topping meringues, providing a cushion of cream for a trifle, or for serving as the base of a fresh fruit fool flavored by whatever is in season. We nearly always eat unsweetened whipped cream in Ireland—and we eat a lot of it.

# POTATO-APPLE CAKE

A favorite autumn dish, Potato-Apple Cake dates back at least to the 18th century. It is made by encasing sweetened apples in a rich potato pastry, and it's a warm dessert for a typically cold, blustery night in Ireland in October or November. In fact, the dense, filling texture means that Potato-Apple Cake makes an excellent harvest supper on its own, served with mugs of mulled cider and glasses of milk.

Serves 4 to 6

For the pastry:

4 medium Idaho potatoes
2 tablespoons butter
1 tablespoon sugar
1 teaspoon salt
½ teaspoon ground ginger
1 cup all-purpose flour (more as needed)

For the filling:

6 large cooking apples, peeled, cored, and
    sliced
3 tablespoons all-purpose flour
¼ cup light brown sugar
3 tablespoons butter
Pinch of nutmeg (optional)
Milk for brushing
sugar for garnish

1   Peel, quarter, and boil the potatoes until tender. Drain and mash the potatoes with the butter, sugar, salt, and ginger, then stir in flour until it makes a pliable dough. (You may need more or less flour depending on your potatoes.) Halve the dough and roll into two circles.

2   Preheat the oven to 375 degrees F and place one half of the dough on a large, well-buttered baking sheet. Cover the dough with apple slices in concentric rings, leaving an inch of pastry border. Sprinkle the apples with flour and sugar and dot with butter. Sprinkle on a bit of nutmeg if desired, and brush the pastry border with a little milk.

3   Cover with the other pastry circle and press to seal. Brush the surface with milk and sprinkle generously with sugar. Cut several vents in the top and place the baking sheet in the oven.

4   Bake for 40 minutes, until the apples are tender and the pastry is golden brown. Serve warm.

## Cooking Apples

The Irish would use Bramley cooking apples for this recipe, large misshapen lumps of apples that bake up beautifully. Use the tartest baking apple you can find, such as Jonagolds, Northern Spy, or Granny Smith. Sprinkle the apple slices with a bit of lemon juice before adding the flour and sugar, to make the flavor tarter.

If serving Potato-Apple Cake as a supper by itself, place each warm slice in a bowl and top with a splash of heavy cream, unsweetened. Eat with a spoon.

# APPLE SNOW

Before the days of global grocery shipping, apples were about the only fresh fruit the Irish could rely on year-round, so recipes for apple desserts have never been in short supply across the country. I think this one is especially good: It's a fluffy little dessert that's not too sweet, is fast to make, and one that really lets the flavor of an heirloom apple shine. I like the tender flesh of a slightly spicy Macoun for this recipe (but it's good even with a sweet Golden Delicious). Traditionally, each diner crumbles a digestive biscuit or two over his or her portion just before eating, but any crumbled cookie—particularly gingersnaps—does the job admirably.

*Makes 4 servings*

**4 cooking apples, peeled, cored, cut into chunks**

**2 tablespoons lemon juice**

**¼ cup sugar**

**2 egg whites**

**¾ cup whipping cream**

**Cookies for crumbs, such as Digestive Biscuits (p. 225) or gingersnaps**

1   Cook the apples in a small saucepan over low heat with the lemon juice and sugar, stirring frequently, until completely cooked down. Purée by pressing through a sieve or simply mashing with a fork to remove any chunks. Cool.

2   Beat the egg whites until stiff and then fold them carefully into the apple purée. Avoid overbeating. Spoon into four glasses and chill.

3   When ready to serve, whip the cream softly and divide among the glasses. Pass whole cookies for each diner to crumble on top before eating.

## Whip It Good

Irish whipped cream is almost never sweetened (unless it's flavored with brandy or whiskey). It can require a little readjustment for American taste buds, but you may come to vastly prefer plain whipped cream, which highlights rather than smothers a dessert. To best approximate Irish-style whipped cream, use organic heavy cream, which will generally have come from grass-fed cows and have more flavor. Whip it softly, by hand, not with a mixer, and dollop it generously onto whatever you're eating.

Not a few Irish people also dollop a spoonful on top of their after-dinner coffee, allowing the cream to melt slowly into the hot coffee while they drink.

# APPLE TART WITH CLOVES

My dad's apple tart was legendary. He had a dab-hand with pastry, whipping up crusts that were light, flaky, and golden, and yet somehow dense and hearty, the perfect foil for sharp-flavored baking apples. He seasoned his tarts only with cloves and sugar, nothing else, so the taste of apples, not cinnamon, was predominant. The old-fashioned recipe for this tart, and the way my dad did it, had whole cloves scattered among the layers to gently infuse the apples with flavor; we simply picked the cloves out as we ate. I still do it that way for grownups, but ground cloves are much more kid-friendly, and that way you can avoid the surprise of biting down on a clove. It's a given that you serve this pie with softly whipped cream, unsweetened.

*Makes 8 servings*

½ cup (1 stick) butter, at room temperature

2 cups all-purpose flour

¼ teaspoon salt

2 eggs

2 to 3 tablespoons cold water

1½ pounds (5 to 6) tart crisp apples, such as Granny Smith, peeled, quartered, cored, and sliced

2/3 cup sugar, plus a little extra for sprinkling

1/8 teaspoon whole cloves or ground cloves

1   Put the flour and salt in the bowl of a food processor. Cut the butter into pieces and add it to the flour. Process until the mixture forms coarse crumbs. Beat one of the eggs with 3 tablespoons cold water. With the machine running, slowly pour this into the food processor. As soon as the dough gathers into a ball, stop adding liquid. Turn the pastry onto a floured surface and divide into two pieces, one consisting of two-thirds of the dough and the other one-third; wrap each in plastic and press to flatten into a round. Refrigerate at least 1 hour and up to 3 days.

2   When ready to bake, adjust the oven rack to lower-middle position and heat oven to 350 degrees F. Toss apples with the sugar and cloves.

3   Roll the larger piece of dough on a floured surface to a 13-inch circle; fit into a 10-inch tart pan or a 9-inch deep-dish pie plate. Turn apples into pie plate. Roll remaining portion of dough on a floured surface into a 10-inch circle. Lay the pastry circle over apples and pinch or press with a fork to seal. Beat the remaining egg with a 1 tablespoon of water and brush the surface of the pastry. Sprinkle with sugar, and decoratively slit the dough top with a paring knife.

4   Bake until pie is golden brown, 45 to 60 minutes. Remove to a wire rack to cool.

# RHUBARB CRUMBLE

What we call "crumble" is what most Americans call a "crisp," and it's one of the desserts where we have a lot of common ground: sweetened fruit underneath a buttery topping of flour and sugar, maybe some oatmeal. Serve it warm with whipped cream, or a spoonful of custard, which we eat a lot in Ireland. I particularly love orange with rhubarb, but you can leave the orange, or stir in 1 to 2 cups sliced fresh strawberries. Melted butter in the topping makes bigger "clumps" of crumble. You can also use this crumble to top 6 cups peeled, cored, and thinly sliced apples tossed with a little sugar and cinnamon.

*Makes 6 servings*
**8 cups sliced rhubarb (from about 2 pounds)**
**¾ cup sugar**
**Juice and zest of one orange**

*For the crumble topping:*
**1 cup rolled oats**
**1 cup all-purpose flour**
**1 cup light brown sugar**
**¼ teaspoon salt**
**½ cup (1 stick) butter, melted**

1   Preheat the oven to 375 degrees F and butter a shallow 2-quart baking dish.

2   Spread the rhubarb slices in the dish and sprinkle with the sugar and orange zest and juice.

3   To make the crumble topping, in a medium bowl, place the dry ingredients, stirring to combine. Pour the melted butter over all and stir to distribute well. Then use your hands to pinch and squeeze the mix to make clumps.

4   Scatter the topping over the rhubarb and bake for 25 to 30 minutes, until the fruit is bubbling and the topping is golden.

# MERINGUES WITH BERRIES AND CREAM

If you have meringues, berries, and cream, you have a summertime dessert that takes seconds to prepare. In grocery stores in Ireland, you can readily buy little meringue rounds, perhaps 4 to 5 inches across, that are just waiting to be topped with whatever berries are freshest and have been macerating in sugar and perhaps a little liqueur, like Irish Mist, if kids are not among the diners. Spoon the juicy berries on top of the meringues, top with a dollop of whipped cream, and you're done. If you don't have an Irish supermarket nearby, however, you'll have to make your own meringues.

*Makes 6 servings*

4 large egg whites
1 cup confectioners' sugar
1 pound fresh berries (raspberries, blueberries, strawberries, blackberries, or a mixture)
1 to 2 tablespoons sugar
1 pint whipping cream

1   Preheat the oven to 300 degrees F and line a rimless baking sheet with parchment paper (a little water or grease under each corner will help it stick).

2   Using an electric mixer, beat the egg whites in a large bowl until frothy. With the beaters running, gradually beat in the confectioners' sugar and continue beating on high until stiff peaks form. Pipe or spoon 6 circles of meringue on the prepared baking sheet, about ¾-inch high and 5 inches in diameter. (You can also make two larger meringues.) Bake for 50 to 55 minutes, until dry but not browned. Turn off the oven and leave the meringues to cool in the cooling oven. When completely cool, you can wrap the meringues tightly in an airtight ziplock bag.

3   An hour before serving, put the berries in a serving dish and spoon a little sugar over them, 1 to 2 tablespoons or to taste. Let them rest, stirring once or twice, to draw some of the juices out. Whip the cream until soft peaks form.

4   For each serving, lay one meringue on a serving plate. Top with a portion of berries and juice, and dollop whipped cream on top. Serve at once.

# CREAMED RICE

"Rice pudding" is such an ordinary name for this dish. I prefer what they call it on the tinned variety at the grocery store: creamed rice, which so much better sums up the unctuous quality of rice baked with cream and sugar. Cook it low and slow and serve it in small portions. It's only lightly sweetened but very rich, a real grownup dessert instead of a kiddy treat, although kids shovel it down like ice cream. I like it chilled as well as warm, so leftovers are never a problem.

*Makes 4 to 6 servings*

2½ cups whole milk

2½ cups light cream

½ cup short-grain rice (use a risotto rice like Arborio)

¼ cup sugar

¼ teaspoon salt

⅛ teaspoon freshly grated nutmeg

¼ cup (½ stick) butter

1   Preheat the oven to 300 degrees F and lightly butter a 2-quart casserole with a lid.

2   Put the milk and cream in the dish and stir in the rice, sugar, salt, and nutmeg. Cut the butter in small pieces and dot it all over the top.

3   Cover the dish and bake for 2 hours, stirring it two or three times during cooking, until the pudding is creamy and thick with a golden-brown top.

# CHOCOLATE SWISS ROLL

This eggy, moist, all but flourless chocolate cake roll looks like a million bucks, but it's surprisingly quick to make and a real favorite among kids, who love both the pinwheel design and the whipped cream filling. The secret to a successful Swiss roll is in rolling it up, parchment paper and all, as soon as it comes out of the oven. That way, you sort of "train" the hot cake to roll. Then you cool it a bit, unroll and peel off the paper liner, slather on whipped cream, and re-roll with ease. If your cake cracks, don't worry. The whipped-cream filling will hold it together long enough to eat it, and if you want it to look prettier, make extra whipped cream and frost the outsides all over to hide the cracks. Cake flour makes a more delicate crumb, but all-purpose flour is fine as well.

Makes 8 servings

3 eggs, at room temperature

⅓ cup sugar

¼ cup cake flour

2 tablespoons unsweetened cocoa powder

1 cup heavy cream

¼ cup confectioners' sugar

1 teaspoon vanilla

To finish:

3 tablespoons confectioners' sugar

1   Preheat the oven to 400 degrees F and grease a 10 x 12-inch rimmed baking sheet (also known as a jelly roll pan). Line the pan with parchment paper or waxed paper, letting several inches of paper overhang either end of the pan, and lightly grease the paper, too (but not the overhang).

2   With an electric mixer in a large bowl, beat the eggs and sugar until thick and lemon colored. Sift the flour and cocoa over the surface and beat just until combined. Spread over the prepared pan, smoothing the batter out to the edges.

3   Bake for 10 minutes, just until the cake is set. Remove from the oven and, using potholders or tea towels to keep from burning your fingers, lift the hot cake in its paper lining onto a clean work surface. Working quickly, sprinkle 2 tablespoons of the confectioners' sugar over the surface and roll up the cake, sugar, paper and all, starting from the short end. Let cool for 10 minutes. Then very gently unroll (it may crack a bit but just let it unroll itself without forcing it), peel off and discard the parchment, and allow the cake to cool to room temperature.

4   Whip the cream with the remaining 2 tablespoons confectioners' sugar and the vanilla, until soft peaks form. While the cake is still barely warm, smooth the whipped cream all over the inside surface. Roll it gently back up. Place it seam-side down on a serving dish and sift the 3 tablespoons confectioners' sugar over the cake. Use a serrated knife and a sawing motion to carefully cut into 8 slices.

# BREAD AND BUTTER PUDDING

This is a decidedly not fancy bread pudding but instead is more of a whimsical, comforting nursery dish. Its main distinction is that the slices of bread are buttered before being layered in the dish. It's ideal for children, who often don't like fancy flavors interfering with the sweet simplicity of a sweet dessert. But even adults will be delighted with the mouthwatering crunch of the edges of toasted bread against the delicate custard. In Ireland, this pudding is, like so many others, served with a spoonful of whipped cream.

Makes 6 servings
8 slices firm-textured white sandwich bread
¼ cup (½ stick) butter, softened
2 tablespoons raisins (optional)
3 eggs
2 cups milk, preferably whole milk
⅓ cup sugar, plus more for sprinkling
2 teaspoons vanilla

1  Preheat the oven to 350 degrees F and butter a 1-quart baking dish. Butter all the bread on one side, right out to the edges, and cut each slice diagonally into 2 triangles.

2  Place the bread triangles in the baking dish cut side downward, arranging the triangles so the pointed tips stand up. Sprinkle with raisins.

3  In a medium bowl, whisk the eggs, then beat in the milk and sugar. Add the vanilla and pour over the bread. Leave to soak for 10 minutes, so the bread can absorb the custard. It's okay if the tips of the bread stick up from the egg and milk; they'll brown nicely and make crunchy spots in the pudding. Sprinkle lightly with sugar so the finished pudding sparkles when it comes out of the oven.

4  Bake for 20 to 25 minutes, until the bread pudding puffs gently and is golden brown. Serve warm.

# RHUBARB FOOL

Fools are old-fashioned desserts of cooked fruit stirred into whipped cream. They shouldn't be too sweet, to let the flavor of the fruit shine through. The sharp and tangy flavor of rhubarb is the perfect complement to the fluffy cream, and the pinkish-green streaks are beautiful, so be careful not to overcook the rhubarb into blandness or mush. Orange zest and juice really brighten the flavor. Let the rhubarb cool completely before swirling it in, and be sure to leave pinky-green streaks of the rhubarb rather than incorporating it completely. If you like, crumble a gingersnap on top of each serving.

*Makes 4 servings*

**3 cups coarsely chopped rhubarb stalks (about 1 pound)**

**¼ cup sugar (or more to taste), plus 2 tablespoons**

**Zest and juice of 1 orange**

**2 cups whipping cream**

**1 teaspoon vanilla**

1   Put the rhubarb, ¼ cup sugar, and the orange juice and zest in a saucepan over medium heat. Bring to a boil and cook, stirring frequently, just until the rhubarb is tender but not until it's pulpy, 6 to 7 minutes. Taste and add a bit more sugar if desired. Remove from the heat and cool completely, mashing slightly with a fork to break up any large chunks.

2   Whip the cream with the 2 tablespoons sugar until soft peaks form. Stir in the vanilla.

3   Pour the cooled rhubarb and their juice over the whipped cream, and fold the fruit in gently, allowing streaks to remain. Cover the bowl with plastic wrap and chill for 2 hours.

4   Spoon into serving bowls or glasses.

## Blueberry Fool

In the spring, all across Ireland, locals know where to go hunting for the wild Irish blueberries known as fraughans (FROCK-ens). But you don't need wild blueberries to enjoy this dessert. You can cook blueberries, raspberries, blackberries, or any other berry you like with a little sugar, and fold into the cream, as above. Gently cook in a large pot over medium heat 2 cups blueberries with ¼ cup sugar (and a little lemon zest, if you like), just until the berries start to pop, 3 to 4 minutes. Let cool completely before swirling into the cream, leaving streaks of purplish berries throughout.

# BAKEWELL TART

As with some Irish food, the name may sound a little British, but the tart is ubiquitous in Ireland. It's a pastry crust with a little bit of raspberry jam in it, topped with a dollop of frangipane (ground almonds creamed with butter, sugar, and egg) and baked until puffed and golden. You can make it as one large tart, but it's more often seen as a finger food, as here. Why so little jam? I don't know. Bakewell tarts are always a little scant on the jam, so if you want authentic, be meager.

1 recipe pastry from Apple Tart (p. 238)
¾ cup (1½ sticks) butter
¾ cup sugar
4 eggs
1½ cups ground almonds
Zest and juice of 1 lemon
¼ cup seedless raspberry jam

1  Preheat the oven 325 degrees F.  Divide the pastry into 18 small balls of dough. Roll each one out to a small circle, and line the bottom of 18 muffin tins. Put the tins in the refrigerator to chill while you make the frangipane.

2  With beaters or standing mixer, cream the butter and sugar until light and fluffy. Separate one of the eggs, reserving the white. Add three whole eggs and the fourth yolk to the butter-sugar and beat until light and creamy. Stir in the ground almonds and lemon juice and zest.

3  Put a dollop of the raspberry jam in the bottom of each pastry-lined tin. Divide the frangipane among the tins.

4  Bake 10 to 12 minutes, until the frangipane is puffed and the pastry is golden. Cool in the muffin tins before gently running a knife around the inside edge of each to remove.

# YELLOWMAN

This famous Irish sweet is immortalized in the song "Did you treat your Mary Ann/ to dulse and yellowman/At the Ould Lammas Fair/ in Ballycastle-oh?" (Dulse is chewy seaweed—Mary Ann must have been a cheap date.) It dates back to the 17th century when it was made for the Lammas Fair, held the last Tuesday in August in Ballycastle, County Antrim. You can still find Yellowman at some country fairs, although with Ireland's thriving confectionery industry, this old-fashioned country sweet is rare.

If you don't want to make your own, you can experience a similar flavor and texture from a "Crunchie," a commercial candy bar with a sort of "yellowman" center dipped in chocolate. They're available as imports in some US shops.

But real Yellowman has a haunting flavor that modern chocolates don't offer. It's crunchy and brittle, like a toffee, but when you suck it for a bit, it becomes chewy in your mouth (in fact, mind your dental work!). True Yellowman is hammered off the larger block with a wooden mallet, so if yours seems very hard, you've probably got it right. Hammered into crumbs, it makes a great topping for ice cream or an addition to cookies.

Makes about 1 pound
**Softened butter**
**1 cup light brown sugar**
**1 16-ounce bottle light corn syrup**
**1 teaspoon baking soda**
**2 tablespoons white vinegar**

1 Grease a 9 × 9-inch baking pan generously with butter.

2 In a large, heavy-sided saucepan, place the sugar, corn syrup, and vinegar over medium heat and stir until the sugar is dissolved. Place a candy thermometer in the mixture and bring it to a boil.

3 Boil, without stirring, until the thermometer registers 290 degrees F.

4 Remove the pan from the heat and stir in the baking soda with a wooden spoon. The mixture will foam up high. Immediately pour it into the prepared pan and smooth with the back of the spoon.

5 Allow to cool and when entirely cold and hard, turn it from the pan and break it into edible pieces with a wooden mallet or a rolling pin.

## Golden Syrup

Yellowman is made with golden syrup, a pure, sugar-cane syrup, rather than the typical American corn syrup. If you can find Lyle's Golden Syrup, a British brand seen in many US supermarkets (it's in a squat green can with gold lettering), use it instead of corn syrup for best flavor.

# BROWN BREAD ICE CREAM

Brown bread shows up at all sorts of meals. But a few years ago, clever pastry chefs figured out how to put it on the dessert table, too: Brown Bread Ice Cream. The ice cream is sometimes flavored with Bailey's Irish Cream liqueur, but you don't need that in order to experience the joy of this unique dish. You don't even need real Irish soda bread! Just toast coarse, whole wheat bread crumbs with a little brown sugar and stir them into softened vanilla ice cream (with a little Bailey's, if you're not feeding kids). The result is nutty, crunchy, caramel-like. It's an instant classic.

Makes 4 to 6 servings

1 pint premium vanilla ice cream
¾ cup coarse whole wheat bread crumbs
3 tablespoons dark brown sugar
Pinch of salt

1  Spoon the pint of ice cream into a mixing bowl and soften the ice cream at room temperature until you can stir it easily. Don't let it melt entirely.

2  While the ice cream is softening, preheat the oven to 375 degrees F and line a small baking sheet with parchment or foil. Spread the crumbs over the foil and sprinkle them with the brown sugar. Take a little pinch of salt, raise your hand a good 8 inches over the crumbs, and sprinkle the salt—the height helps distribute it better.

3  Toast the crumbs in the oven for 8 to 10 minutes, stirring once or twice, until they're toasty, brown and crisp. Remove and let cool completely. Reserve two tablespoons for topping.

4  Stir the remaining cooled crumbs into the ice cream and freeze until firm. Serve scoops with a light sprinkle of the reserved crumbs.

# IRISH TRIFLE

Old-fashioned trifles in the 19th century were sumptuous affairs, big bowls of homemade cake cubes doused in sherry, fresh summer fruit, custard, and cream. Modern Irish trifle is a little more prosaic—usually cake cubes and canned fruit cocktail with jelly (what Americans call Jello) poured over the cake and chilled before it's covered in readymade custard and cream—but no less beloved for all that. This festive trifle is a happy medium between the two: Store-bought pound cake and fresh fruit, homemade custard and freshly whipped cream. You can make it in one big glass bowl or in little individual dishes as you prefer.

*Makes 8 servings*

**4 cups fresh berries (blueberries, sliced strawberries, raspberries, or a combination)**

**2 tablespoons sugar**

**2 tablespoons sherry or Irish whiskey, or more to taste (optional)**

**1 16-ounce pound cake, diced into ¾-inch cubes**

For the custard:

**½ cup sugar**

**3 tablespoons cornstarch**

**3 cups whole milk**

**4 egg yolks**

**2 teaspoons vanilla**

**3 tablespoons butter**

To finish:

**2 cups whipping cream**

**2 tablespoons sugar**

**1 teaspoon vanilla**

1   Toss the berries with the sugar and sherry or whiskey, if using. Set aside for 10 minutes, stirring a couple times to let the sugar draw the juices out of the fruit.

2   In 8 glass dishes or one large glass bowl, layer the cake cubes. Spoon on the fruit and its syrup to douse the cake. (If you like, this is the time to sprinkle on a little more sherry or whiskey, but don't soak it.)

3   In a large, heavy saucepan over medium heat, whisk the sugar and cornstarch. Slowly whisk in the milk to prevent lumps forming, then beat in the egg yolks. Bring to a boil, stirring constantly, and cook, stirring constantly for 3 to 4 minutes, until thickened. Remove from the heat and stir in the butter and vanilla. Set aside to cool slightly.

4   While the custard cools, whip the cream with the sugar and vanilla till soft peaks form. Pour the custard over the cake and fruit, then top with the whipped cream. Cover and chill for at least 2 hours before serving, or as long as overnight, to let the flavors meld.

# CHRISTMAS PLUM PUDDING

If you don't have an Auntie Mary to make your Christmas pudding for you, the way I do, you'll have to make your own. It's a better option than buying one of those tiny, outrageously expensive ones you sometimes see in gourmet stores—they're not very good anyway. The holiday pud used to be made with suet, but butter has long since replaced it in many households. It makes a pudding lighter in both taste and color, and I infinitely prefer it. It's traditional to invite everyone in the house, including any guests, into the kitchen to take a turn stirring the pudding with a wooden spoon after all the ingredients are in. It's supposed to bring luck on the household and the pudding. Ideally, you are supposed to make this pudding a month in advance of the holiday, but in America, I've made it as little as three days before Christmas. I'm sure we missed some complexity and maturity of flavors—but we didn't care.

*Makes 24 servings*

1 cup light brown sugar
Grated zest and juice of 1 orange
Grated zest and juice of 1 lemon
1 cup dried currants
1 cup golden raisins
1 cup dark raisins
½ cup candied cherries
½ cup candied peel
1 12-ounce bottle Guinness Extra
  Stout
1 cup soft white bread crumbs
1 cup all-purpose flour

2 teaspoons ground cinnamon
1 teaspoon allspice
½ teaspoon freshly grated nutmeg
½ teaspoon ground cloves
½ teaspoon ground ginger
1 cup (2 sticks) butter, softened
4 eggs, lightly beaten
1 small apple, peeled, cored, and
  shredded
½ cup sliced almonds
Brandy for drizzling (optional)
Lightly sweetened whipped cream,
  flavored with brandy (if you like),
  for serving

1  Put the sugar, the orange and lemon zest, and all the dried fruit, candied cherries, and candied peel in a large bowl and pour the bottle of Guinness over everything, stirring to combine. Cover the bowl with a plate and leave it to sit overnight at room temperature.

2  The next day, in another large bowl, combine the bread crumbs and flour with all the spices. Add the butter and either cut it in with a pastry cutter, or do as traditional Irish cooks do and rub it in with your fingers. (This does work well, but I highly recommend taking off your rings first!)

3  Stir the eggs, grated apple, and almonds into the fruit and Guinness, then pour the wet ingredients into the dry ingredients and stir to combine.

(This is the part where you invite everyone to take a few stirs for luck.)

4   Grease a large pudding bowl with butter. You probably don't have a pudding bowl, per se, but a 2-quart Pyrex—or other heatproof—bowl is ideal. Pour in the pudding mixture and cover the top with parchment paper and foil, pressing it down tightly around the rim. Tie a couple of rounds of kitchen string under the rim, and fashion a handle by tying a couple more pieces of string across the top, leaving enough slack so you can use it to pick up the bowl if necessary. (More important than picking it up is the extra insurance the top will stay on while the pudding boils.) Modern plastic pudding bowls have a fitted lid, but I don't love boiling plastic, even the heatproof kind, for 3 hours when there's something I'm going to eat inside.

5   Put the heatproof bowl in the bottom of a large stockpot and pour in water to come a little more than halfway up the sides of the bowl. Put it on the stove, bring the water to a boil over medium heat, and simmer gently for 3 hours, topping off the water from time to time. It helps to drop a few glass marbles or small round pebbles in the water—as the water gets low, they'll rattle around to alert you to add more water.

6   After 3 hours, you can either lift out the pudding with your improvised handle (be careful!) or, better, let the pudding cool in the water and then lift it out.

7   Take off the wrapping and, if you like, poke a few holes in the top with a skewer and drizzle a few tablespoons of brandy over the pudding. Cover it up with fresh parchment and foil and refrigerate until Christmas Day. (In the British Isles, it would be left on a high shelf in the pantry, but they generally keep their houses cooler than Americans do, so we're better off refrigerating the pudding to avoid any risk of mold.) If you're "feeding" your pudding with brandy, drizzle on a little more every week. You can store your pudding for a good month or more before Christmas.

8   When you're ready to serve, reboil the pudding as above for 1 hour to heat it through. (I've heard you can remove the foil and microwave it on medium for half an hour, but I've never done it myself; no reason why it shouldn't work though.) Heat a little brandy, maybe 1/3 cup, briefly in a small saucepan (cold brandy won't light, no matter how many matches you hold to the surface), then set it alight with a match, pour the burning liquid over the pudding, and carry it, flaming, to the table. The liquor quickly burns itself out, but the show is incomparable! Slice up the warm pudding and top each piece with a dollop of cold, lightly sweetened whipped cream, with or without brandy flavoring.

# MINCEMEAT

Even in Ireland, many of us tend to buy our mincemeat these days. It's partly that we may have forgotten to plan ahead—it has to mature for at least three weeks—and also that store versions can be so good. Because we tend not to have cool dark pantries in America, when I make my own mincemeat, I store it in the refrigerator. This version makes a good quart, enough for a round of mini mince pies (p. 265), and also for a mince tart. The only challenge may be finding the suet, but larger supermarkets usually have it at Christmastime. Tightly sealed, this will stay good in the fridge for months.

*Makes about 4 cups*
½ cup dark brown sugar
½ cup shredded beef suet
½ cup raisins
½ cup golden raisins
½ cup currants
¼ cup Irish whiskey
¼ cup mixed peel
1 large green apple, such as Granny Smith, peeled, cored, and diced very small
Juice and zest of 1 lemon
2 tablespoons orange marmalade
¼ teaspoon freshly grated nutmeg

1   Mix all the ingredients in a large bowl, stirring well to combine. Pack into a quart-size glass jar, pressing a circle of parchment paper onto the surface to keep air off it. Seal and refrigerate for at least 3 weeks before using to let the flavors mellow and mature.

## Brandy Butter and Cream

Plain whipped cream is good enough for us all year 'round, but come the holidays, we want a little more, and that usually entails some brandy (or whiskey) in the whipped cream or perhaps some brandy butter. We're a cream family at my house, but some people swear by brandy butter. Christmas hampers—large food-filled gift baskets—will sometimes contain a little jar of artisan brandy butter.

To make brandy cream to top your pudding or mince pie, beat 1 cup of whipping cream until soft peaks form, and then gently beat in 3 tablespoons confectioners' sugar and 3 tablespoons brandy. Double or triple this recipe and repeat as needed from December 24th to January 1st.

To make brandy butter, a slather of which will melt temptingly on top of a slab of warm Christmas pudding, soften 1/2 cup butter and whip it till smooth. Then beat in 3 tablespoons granulated sugar and 3 tablespoons brandy. You can substitute Irish whiskey in either recipe, but brandy has a smoother flavor.

# MINCE PIES

You do not have to make mincemeat to make a mincemeat pie. Even ordinary American supermarkets stock jars or Tetrapak boxes of mincemeat around Christmastime. Buy the base ready-made and then dress it up by adding goodies such as extra orange zest and juice along with some dried fruit like cherries or cranberries, for a tart burst of chewiness. And while it would be nice, of course, to make a buttery, homemade short-crust pastry to encase it, it's also a lot easier to thaw out a roll of phyllo dough and use that instead. This way, you can have wonderful pastries that, for all intents and purposes, are homemade, with a lot less fuss.

Be sure to read the label when you purchase mincemeat! Some packages of mincemeat are intended to be reconstituted with water or orange juice, so if the mincemeat seems dry and crumbly, make sure you follow the package instructions so you're starting with 2 cups of "finished" mincemeat before you add any additional ingredients.

*Makes 2 dozen tarts*

**2 cups mincemeat**
**¼ cup dried cherries or cranberries**
**Grated zest and juice of 1 orange**
**¼ teaspoon ground cloves**
**17 ounces frozen phyllo pastry, thawed**
**½ cup (1 stick) butter, melted**
**Confectioners' sugar, for garnish**
**Whipped cream, for serving**

1   Preheat the oven to 375 degrees F and lightly grease two 12-cup muffin tins. Put the mincemeat in a bowl and stir in the dried cherries, orange zest and juice, and cloves.

2   Lay a sheet of phyllo on a clean work surface, and cover the remaining phyllo with a clean dish towel to keep it from drying out. Using a pastry brush, brush melted butter on the sheet, and continue layering and brushing with butter until you have about 8 sheets stacked up. Cut the stack into 6 squares, and push each buttered, stacked square down into a muffin cup, letting the edges stand upright. Repeat with more phyllo until all the muffin tins are filled.

3   Put a heaping tablespoon of mincemeat into the center of each phyllo-lined cup. Bake for 20 to 22 minutes, until the mincemeat is bubbling and the phyllo is golden brown and crisp.

4   When all the mincemeat tarts are baked, sift confectioners' sugar generously over them and serve them warm, dropping a spoonful of whipped cream on top of each just before it's going to be eaten (if you let it sit, the cream will melt and the phyllo won't be crisp!).

# IRISH CHOCOLATE TRUFFLES

Is this a classic Irish dessert? It is nowadays. For some reason—perhaps simply that all Europeans *really* like good chocolate—Ireland has become host to some exceptional homegrown chocolatiers, and Irish-owned grocery stores such as Superquinn have chocolate aisles that are wonderful to behold. I'll try anything at least once, and probably more than that, when it's wrapped in packaging that suggests a craftsman rather than a corporation made it. By searching out such packaging, I've gotten to eat some truly exquisite chocolate. I think one of the best ways to savor a good chocolate, especially a potent dark one, is in an after-dinner truffle. You see After Eight dinner mints at parties all over Ireland, but increasingly, you see artisan or homemade truffles, too. Make these with the finest chocolate you can manage. If you're shopping in American supermarkets, Ghirardelli or Scharffen Berger will produce excellent results.

*Makes about 4 dozen truffles*

**2/3 cup heavy cream**

**8 ounces good-quality dark chocolate**

**1 cup unsweetened cocoa powder**

1 Bring the cream just to a boil in a saucepan. Immediately remove it from the heat and break the chocolate pieces into the hot cream. Stir gently to melt them.

2 Scrape the mixture into a bowl and let it stand in a cool place until firm, 1 to 2 hours. If the temperature in your kitchen is very warm, you can put it in the refrigerator, but check it every 5 minutes or so and don't let it chill into complete stiffness. It should still be pliable.

3 Line a baking sheet with parchment paper. Use a pair of small teaspoons (or your buttered hands) to form the chocolate mixture into very small balls, no larger than about 3/4 inch. Then deposit the balls on the parchment, smoothing the edges with your fingertips without overworking the chocolate.

4 Put the cocoa in a shallow bowl. Working in batches, toss the truffles gently in the cocoa. Store them in an airtight container in the refrigerator for up to 2 weeks. You can toss them again in cocoa just before serving. (They also look nice set into individual mini cupcake papers.)

## Whipped Syllabubs

Take a quart of very thick cream half a pint of white wine the juice of three lemons, the peel of one of them grated and thrown in sweeten it with loaf sugar to your taste mix all together in an earthen pan then beat it all one way with a whisk till it is so thick that a rod may stand on it, then take it off by spoonfulls and fill your glasses it may stand a night in the pan before you glass them up it will then keep a week.

—from an 18th century Irish cookbook manuscript

We do drink a lot of tea, I suppose. I never really thought about it until I went back to live in Ireland for a while after having been in America for years. Though in the States my wife drank coffee, when we moved to Ireland, we switched to tea. We had the kettle constantly on the boil because we had a lot of visitors calling in, either old friends or family, or new friends and acquaintances in our new village, wanting to get a look at "the Yanks up at the cottage." (The fact that I am Irish was all but negated by the fact that my wife was not.) She loved it, and kept a tin of biscuits and a flowery teapot ready for all and sundry, and hardly anyone said no, including deliverymen who were merely bringing a load of turf to keep us warm in that cottage without a furnace.

We drank so much tea during the day that first autumn, and pints of Guinness at the various local pubs at night, that it was quite a while before I remembered the pleasures of other Irish drinks: like elderflower lemonade in the summer, a hot port in the pub on a raw wintry night, and a milk punch for the mornings after.

And lemon barley water, which you can buy in the grocery store and dilute at home, or make yourself by soaking barley in water with lemon zest. "Why do you drink barley water?" my wife wanted to know, dubiously eyeing the cloudy liquid. It has all sorts of health claims: tonic, refresher, reliever of "weak kidneys." But the truth is, I think, we just like it.

# LEMON BARLEY WATER

If you love it, you don't have to ask why. But if you're unaccustomed to it, the cloudy look may surprise you. It's kind of like very mild lemonade; the barley imparts body. Barley water tastes rich, somehow, and it's restorative. Many decades ago, it was a sort of early sports drinks, given to athletes or brought to farmers working in the fields. Give it a try. This recipe makes a small amount, and if you like it, you can double it easily. You can also sweeten it with honey instead of sugar.

For 2 servings
2 lemons
¼ cup pearl barley
3 cups water
⅓ cup sugar (or to taste)

1   Trim the zest off the lemons in long strips, avoiding the bitter white pith. Put the strips of zest in a medium saucepan with the barley and the water. Squeeze the lemon juice into a cup and reserve.

2   Bring to a boil, reduce heat, and simmer gently for half an hour, until the barley is soft. Strain out and discard the barley and zest.

3   Stir in the reserved lemon juice and sugar to taste. Chill before drinking. Store in a glass bottle or jar in the refrigerator for up to three days.

# ELDERFLOWER LEMONADE

Elder bushes grow abundantly in Ireland, and each summer, their branches are heavy with big clusters of tiny, creamy flowers. Their distinctive perfume is heady and vaguely citrus-like without being overpowering, and it's frequently used as a flavoring in desserts and beverages (it pairs deliciously with apple juice) and to make homemade wine. In the United States, elderflowers are more commonly seen in northern climates such as Vermont and New Hampshire. If you're fortunate enough to have elderflowers, try this lemonade, a drink that shows up in Irish restaurants and cafes each summer. If not, follow the directions below using 8 elderflower herbal tea bags.

Makes about 2 quarts
2 quarts water
3-4 elderflower clusters, picked over and washed
2 cups sugar (or to taste)
Juice of 6 lemons

1   Place the water and elderflowers in a saucepan and bring to a boil, pushing the flowers down into the water with a wooden spoon. Turn off the heat and leave the flowers soaking for 20 minutes. Remove the flowers with a slotted spoon and discard them.

2   Put the sugar into the hot water and stir until dissolved. Refrigerate until very cold.

3   To serve, stir in the fresh lemon juice and taste to adjust for sugar. Serve over ice, perhaps with a sprig of fresh elderflower tucked into each glass for decoration. Store covered in the refrigerator for up to a week.

# HOT WHISKEY

When my wife was expecting our first child, we went back to visit friends in Graiguenamanagh, the village in County Kilkenny where we lived for a time. She caught a bad cold but was 6 months pregnant and didn't want to take any medications. I took her to the kindly village doctor whom we used to see occasionally when we lived there. He listened to her concerns and snorted, "You Americans! You're so uptight! Go down to the pub now and have a hot whiskey, and you'll feel better straightaway." On doctor's advice, off we went to our favorite local, as your preferred pub is known, and, as my wife tells it, "I did, and I did!"

For one serving

**8 whole cloves**

**1 slice lemon, ¼-inch thick**

**1 jigger Irish whiskey (1½ ounces or 3 tablespoons)**

**¾ cup boiling water**

**1 teaspoon white sugar (or to taste)**

1   Press cloves into the triangles of the lemon flesh and put the piece in the bottom of a heavy tumbler or wine glass. Pour the whiskey on top of it.

2   Put a metal spoon in the glass and pour the boiling water in so the stream hits the bowl of the spoon. Add sugar to taste and drink hot. Bartenders sometimes serve the sugar and a spoon on the side, and nearly always twist a paper napkin around the glass so you can pick it up while it's still very hot.

## Hot Port

Fragrant and soothing on a cold, raw day, hot port is prepared like hot whiskey but with a double shot of a good quality port instead and usually no sugar. When you order a hot port in a pub in Ireland, the bartender nearly always says, "With or without sugar?" because generally port is sweet enough without it.

# IRISH COFFEE

Maybe it was invented for tourists by a chef at a restaurant at Shannon Airport, as the story goes, but nobody cares; we all drink it, you can get it anywhere, and it's the one surefire food of Ireland that practically anyone in the world can name. I've been at many an Irish dinner party where Irish Coffee was served after dinner, and I think it's because hosts love the tableside drama of floating the cream.

This is important: Irish Coffee is made with only very lightly whipped cream, but American cream has a lower butterfat content so it helps to whip it till it's nearly making soft peaks. Real pros in Ireland (read: bartenders) don't whip it at all, but anything you can do to make it work helps. The goal is to make the cream float so it looks like the foam on a pint of Guinness. You hold a spoon upside down over sweetened coffee and slowly pour cream over it so it floats on the surface. The amount of cream partly depends on the shape of the glass: you want a visible white line, so a wide glass requires more cream. The coffee can't be too hot or the cream will just melt into it (hot, yes, but not piping hot; let it cool a few minutes), and it must be sweetened. That tablespoon of sugar—you can use more, but not less—keeps the cream afloat.

For one serving

2 to 4 tablespoons whipping cream
1 cup strong, freshly brewed coffee
1 tablespoon sugar (or more to taste, but not less)
1 jigger Irish whiskey (1½ ounces or 3 tablespoons)

1  Whisk the cream until it starts to thicken. If you actually whip it stiff, it won't flow over the spoon and spread over the surface, so just beat until soft peaks begin to form.

2  Ideally, use a footed Irish coffee glass, or a thick wineglass or glass mug. Fill about 3/4 full with coffee that's not super hot. Stir in the whiskey and sugar. (The whiskey cools the coffee a bit if you're in doubt.)

3  Hold a teaspoon upside down and horizontally over the glass with the tip of it not quite touching the coffee. Slowly drizzle the cream over the spoon. It should flow off the tip and slowly spread across the surface of the coffee rather than plunging to the bottom.

# BLACK VELVET

Guinness is considered by its many aficionados to be extremely creamy, but when you add it to champagne or prosecco, its fruitiness emerges as well. The proportions are roughly two parts bubbly to one part Guinness, but you can mix it to taste. It's a bit of a novelty drink, but, like Irish Coffee, it's found all over Ireland. Black Velvet is a terrific party drink. It's Irish, you can mix it to order as guests arrive, it's delicious—and it stretches your Champagne farther!

*For one serving*

**4 ounces (½ cup) chilled Champagne or prosecco**
**2 ounces (¼ cup) chilled Guinness Extra Stout**

1   Pour the champagne into a flute or other tall glass.

2   Pour the Guinness on top. (Guinness is heavier. If you mix it the other way around, it won't combine evenly and will need to be stirred.)

# GUINNESS AND BLACKCURRANT

Some pubs still have snugs, but you might never know it unless you're a local. That's because they're so well hidden from the main part of the pub. They were originally for private meetings, or the clergy or local gentry, but they were also for women to have a drink in privacy. Say the local chatelaine fancied a whiskey or a pint after the hunt, she could drink it either in the privacy of her carriage, or car, or, more comfortably, in the snug. The days are long gone when ladies were not welcome in the bar (they weren't banned so much as frowned upon and invited to move to the lounge), but even so, Guinness and Blackcurrant is mainly considered a ladies' drink that men would rarely order. That said, we do drink it! For those who don't like the dryness or bitterness of Guinness, you can take the edge off with a shot of blackcurrant cordial. You just have to ask.

*For one serving*

**1 to 2 tablespoons blackcurrant cordial or liqueur (or to taste)**
**1 pint Guinness**

1   Pour the blackcurrant into the center of the pint and swirl it (don't stir!) to combine.

# MILK PUNCH

Cold milk punch, as with any milk punch (see Eggnog below), is meant to be restorative. The cold version is more for someone "with a head on him," as we might say of someone who'd indulged a bit much at the pub the night before. The sufferer might say, "Give us a milk punch there. I've quite the head on me." And here's what the bartender would mix, with a tiny shot of dark rum, or "black rum," as we call it in Ireland. From experience, we're big believers in the efficacy of the hair of the dog. You'll hear there's no ice in Irish bars. There is. You just have to ask for it.

For one serving

½ cup whole milk

1 jigger Irish whiskey or brandy (1½ ounces or 3 tablespoons)

½ jigger dark rum (¾ ounce or 1½ tablespoons)

1 teaspoon sugar (or to taste)

Freshly grated nutmeg

1   Mix all the ingredients in a tumbler. Add a couple ice cubes and stir vigorously to chill. Top with a grating of nutmeg.

# EGGNOG (HOT MILK PUNCH)

Eggnog for Ireland is not so much a festive holiday tipple as a warm and comforting restorative for invalids or those under the weather. You might whip up an eggnog to sooth the nerves of someone who's had a shock. Here's how.

For one serving

1 cup whole milk

1 egg

1 tablespoon sugar (or to taste)

1 jigger brandy or Irish whiskey (1½ ounces or 3 tablespoons)

Freshly grated nutmeg

1   Heat the milk in a small saucepan to just short of boiling. While the milk heats, whisk the egg briskly with the sugar in a large mug.

2   Pour the milk slowly over the egg and sugar mixture, whisking constantly. Stir in the brandy or whisky, and top with nutmeg.

# SLOE GIN

In the autumn, sloes ripen all over the Irish countryside. They're actually a type of tiny dark blue and hard wild plum, but if you try to eat one off the bush, they're tart and mouth-puckering. Poked all over with a needle, gathered in the bottom of a bottle, and topped with gin, however, they slowly release their flavor, imparting a subtle fruitiness and, beautifully, a glowing crimson to the gin. Sloes may be near impossible to find in America. (If you're lucky enough to live near a dune and you can gather beach plums, try them instead.) Make more than one bottle in the autumn when the sloes are ripe. Otherwise you'll be very sorry later. You can sip it on the rocks as an aperitif. Make a Sloe Gin and Tonic, or try a Sloe Gin Fizz: 2 jiggers sloe gin, 1 tablespoon lemon juice, and 1/2 cup soda water.

To make 1 quart

4 cups gin
4 cups sloes
1 cup sugar

1   Use a large sewing needle to prick the sloes. (You can do this in a slapdash manner, poking at the mass of sloes, rather than trying to prick each one.)

2   Divide the sloes between two quart-size glass jars, and pour half the gin into each. Divide the sugar among the two jars, seal the jar, and shake well.

3   Let the sloe gin rest for 3 to 4 months, shaking the bottles occasionally. I've never had it last long enough to bother straining out the sloes and bottling the gin separately, but perhaps you'll do better.

# APPLE MEAD

I can't claim this is a drink that's known all over Ireland, but it's a quirky and interesting one that pays homage to a lot of Irish beverages, including mead, the fermented honey drink the Irish monks made. Despite its sweet and innocuous name, this drink kicks like a mule. With champagne (or prosecco), a little apple cider (you can use hard cider or regular cider, as you prefer), a taste of honey, and a dash of Irish whiskey, it's delicious and goes down easy. But in potency, it reminds me of a French 75, the cocktail of champagne, lemon juice, simple syrup, and brandy. It, too, slips down with ease, but a short time later you realize why it was named after French guns in World War I.

For 1 serving

1½ ounces (3 tablespoons) apple cider (soft or hard, as you prefer)

1 jigger Irish whiskey (1½ ounces or 3 tablespoons)

1 teaspoon honey

4 ounces (½ cup) Champagne or prosecco

1  Put the cider, whiskey, and honey in a cocktail shaker with crushed ice and shake.

2  Strain into a large martini glass and top with the Champagne.

## To Make Walnut Catchup

Take half a peck of walnuts before they be hard shelled, and stamp them in a mortar, put them into an earthen pot with half a pound of salt, stir them every day for six weeks then press the liquor off, and to every quart put cloves, mace, ginger, nutmeg white and black pepper each one dram, and an quarter of an ounce of shallots, boil them in an quarter of an hour, then put it into a pot and cover it and let it stand ten days then strain it off and put to it half a pint of wine and a quarter of a pound of anchovies, boil it ten minutes when it is cold bottle it off.

—from an 18th century Irish cookbook manuscript

Making marmalades, jams, and preserves is a time-honored autumn activity, and slovenly was the homemaker who wasn't making her marmalade herself. (In fact, at my house, it was my dad who took jam-making very seriously—so much for old stereotypes!) Nowadays, there are excellent, high-quality jams and marmalades readily available at any store, and it seems every Christmas brings a new hamper full of beautiful jars of chutneys and preserves. But not all store-bought jam is good, of course. I try to buy jars with labels saying the contents were made by hand in someone's farm kitchen down the country.

Or, I make it myself. The only way to truly know what's in your jam is to do it at home, and making small batches is fast and surprisingly easy. It only becomes an enormous kitchen melodrama if you're trying to process fifteen or twenty pounds of fruit. My rule of thumb is to prepare only enough of something to store in the refrigerator, making a few cups at a time. If you're only making two cups of jam, it's no big deal, and you get to skip the arduous steps of canning and processing.

# ORANGE MARMALADE

Seville oranges are preferred for marmalade because they have the perfect blend of citrus and bitterness. Good marmalade—unlike, say, good strawberry jam—should be much more than one-note sweetness. That edge of bitterness—not too much, not too little—is highly prized by marmalade lovers.

In Ireland, you can buy large tins of cooked-down fruit you turn into a pan, add sugar, and cook into many, many jars of marmalade or jam. That's because it's the prepping of the fruit that can take so long. Even in this recipe, the oranges must be boiled for a long time to soften the rind. A good rule to remember for jam-making is slow-cooking before adding the sugar, fast boiling after. Then your final product tastes fresh and fruity, not "cooked" and sugary.

Seville oranges do show up in American markets, at high prices, for about five minutes every year. If you miss that window, substitute three oranges and a lemon, or a small pink grapefruit to get the hint of bitterness. It's a good and workable substitute.

Makes about 3½ cups
1 pound (about 5 or 6) Seville oranges (or 5 Valencia or other thin-skinned oranges and 1 lemon or small pink grapefruit)
4 cups sugar

1   Scrub the rind of the fruit and put it, whole, into a large saucepan with cold water to cover. Bring to a boil over high heat, and then reduce heat slightly and simmer rapidly, topping up the water now and then as needed, for about two hours, until the oranges are soft and the rind can easily be pierced with a fork.

2   Lift the cooked oranges out of the cooking liquid, keeping the liquid in the pot. Let the oranges cool enough to handle. Then cut them up and discard the seeds and any large hunks of membrane. Chop all the flesh, catching and reserving as much juice as you can, and slice the rind up into fine shreds (or slightly thicker chunks if you prefer your marmalade that way).

3   Return all the chopped fruit and juices to the cooking liquid and cook at a medium boil over medium-high heat until the liquid has reduced by about one third and, more importantly, the temperature has reached 222 degrees F. A candy and jam thermometer that stays in the pot is immensely useful (and inexpensive), but you can also keep testing with an instant-read thermometer. It will hover just below 222 for a long time, maybe 15 or 20 minutes, as the water evaporates. Just keep an eye on it as the temperature will suddenly shoot upward.

4   While the fruit is cooking, preheat the oven to 200 degrees F and spread the sugar on a rimmed baking sheet. Heat the sugar while the fruit cooks, just to heat it through but not melt (see Heating Sugar p. 290).

5   Carefully add the hot sugar to the pot and bring it to a rapid boil. Cook hard for 20 to 25 minutes, until the marmalade sets. You can tell it has set when a teaspoon of marmalade on a saucer makes a wrinkled skin as you blow on it. Ladle into two clean glass pint jars and cool completely before sealing and storing in the refrigerator where it will stay good for 6 months or longer.

# BLACKCURRANT JAM

I see blackcurrants for sale in gourmet markets sometimes in the United States, and they're so expensive I shelve my jam dreams again for a while. We eat a lot of blackcurrants in Ireland, where they grow very well; so many people have a bush, or several, in their back gardens. Redcurrants are milder and tarter, but fresh blackcurrants already taste like jam even when they're fresh. When they become jam, the result is intense: deep, dark purple, darker than grape jelly, with a strong, tart sweetness and a memorable, lasting flavor.

*Makes about 3 cups*

**4 cups fresh blackcurrants, picked over, stems removed**

**1 cup water**

**3 cups sugar**

1  Preheat the oven to 200 degrees F. Spread the sugar on a rimmed baking sheet and put it in the oven to heat.

2  Put the blackcurrants and water in a large saucepan over medium heat. Bring to a simmer, and cook for 15 to 20 minutes, until tender.

3  Stir the heated sugar into the jam. Raise the heat to medium high and bring the jam to a boil. Boil rapidly, stirring several times, for 5 minutes. Spoon the jam into two clean jars and cool completely. Store in the refrigerator for up to a month.

## Heating Sugar

Experienced Irish jam makers always heat their sugar before adding it to the fruit. The reasoning is that hot sugar added to the already cooking fruit doesn't delay the process. It brings the boiling jam to temperature much quicker so it can set faster and the fruit doesn't have that overcooked taste some jams have. And in a side-by-side taste test, you truly can tell the difference between, say, strawberry jam that was long-boiled with its "cooked" jammy taste, and the fresh, berry-ish strawberry flavor of jam made with heated sugar, which boiled for no longer than five minutes. To heat sugar, preheat the oven to 200 degrees F, spread the sugar on a rimmed baking sheet, and heat for 15 to 20 minutes, until hot through but not at all melted.

BLACKCURRANT, July 2011 JAM

# RASPBERRY JAM

When I was growing up, my father kept a big garden where raspberries grew particularly well. We were never short of them, to eat with sugar and cream, to top meringues or tarts, or to make jam. Like strawberry jam, raspberry jam is almost laughably simple: berries, sugar, a squeeze of lemon. The only difficulty—and you may not consider it a problem—is that it's so full of seeds. I don't like raspberry jam completely seedless, but I do like it a little less seedy, so I strain half the jam through a fine metal sieve. This recipe goes light on the sugar. If you want it sweeter, add up to another cup of sugar during cooking.

Makes about 3½ cups
**6 cups fresh red raspberries**
**2 cups sugar**
**Juice of 1 lemon**

1   Put the berries in a wide, heavy-bottomed saucepan and mash them coarsely with a potato masher.

2   Place the pot over medium heat and bring to a boil. Cook it hard for 1 to 2 minutes, then stir in the sugar.

3   Return to a boil and cook for 4 to 5 minutes, stirring constantly. Remove from the heat and stir in the lemon juice.

4   If you like, strain half (or all) the jam through a metal sieve, pushing the jam through with the back of a spoon and discarding the seeds. You may have to scrape and stir in the sieve to move the jam along. If you're only straining half the jam, stir the strained jam back into the pot.

5   Divide the jam between two clean pint jars (it won't quite fill them). Allow to cool, cover tightly, and store in the refrigerator for up to four weeks.

## Bramble Jelly

In October, all along the roads in Ireland, the brambles, as we call blackberries, have ripened in the hedgerows. You can stop your car on a country road and pluck a whole bucketful of them in a very short time. An apple is a typical addition, bringing some much-needed natural pectin to what would otherwise be quite a runny jam. Pushing it through a metal sieve is important because otherwise it's too seedy.

Makes about 2 cups
**1 pound ripe blackberries**
**1 sweet apple, peel on**
**⅓ cup water**
**2 cups sugar**

1   Put the berries in a large, heavy saucepan. Cut the apple into quarters, discarding the core and seeds, and put the quarters into the pan. Add the water and bring to a boil. Reduce heat and simmer gently until the fruit is soft—so soft the apple peel comes off the quarters, 30 to 40 minutes.

2   Push the fruit through a metal sieve into a clean medium saucepan, being sure to scrape all the purée off the bottom of the sieve. Stir in the sugar and bring to a boil over medium heat. Boil the jam hard until it starts to thicken, 10 to 15 minutes. Turn into a clean pint jar and let cool. Keep in the refrigerator for up to a month.

# STRAWBERRY JAM

Irish strawberries are so sweet. Apparently berries don't like a lot of sun and do like a lot of rain, because what we lack in tomatoes and basil and melons, we more than make up for in raspberries, blackberries, red and blackcurrants, and strawberries. True Irish-grown strawberries are, of course, seasonal, but the short period in summer when they're flowing through markets is the perfect time to make this jam, which is super easy. Keep it in the fridge for several months to spread on scones with a dollop of cream. This is a soft and runny jam, more like a conserve, without pectin and all the more natural tasting for it. I do not boil it until it "sets" because I prefer the fresher flavor. Stirring in lemon juice at the very end brightens the taste and keeps the jam from being cloying. If you want a firmer jam, boil it for as long as 15 minutes in Step 3, until a teaspoon on a saucer forms a wrinkled "skin" on top when you blow on it.

*Makes about 3½ cups*

**6 cups sliced fresh strawberries**
**¼ cup water**
**2½ cups sugar**
**Juice of 1 lemon**

1   Hull the strawberries, slicing them if they're large, and place them in a large saucepan. Crush them roughly with a potato masher.

2   Stir in the water and place the pan over medium-low heat. As the juices begin to flow, increase the heat slightly to bring the strawberries to a gentle simmer. A pinkish-gray scum will begin to rise. Use a wide metal spoon to lift it off onto a saucer. At our house, this is the cook's treat, to be shared with any passing children (and you may be surprised how many children start to pass through the kitchen as the smell of strawberry jam begins to float through the house).

3   When the scum stops rising, add the sugar (heated or not, as you prefer) and bring to a rolling boil. Cook it hard at full boil for about 5 minutes, then remove from the heat and stir in the juice of the lemon. Ladle into two clean glass pint jars. Cool completely before sealing and storing in the refrigerator for up to two months.

# RHUBARB AND GINGER JAM

Every spring, big pink stalks of rhubarb begin to appear on market stalls with signs that say, "Irish Rhubarb" and "Irish-grown!" We prize rhubarb highly for crumbles (p. 240) and jams, and we feel strongly the local stuff is best. Many families have a rhubarb patch in their gardens, and it's one of the most rewarding things you can grow. Once it's established, you don't have to do anything to it, and every year it comes back again and again, a veritable dessert plant giving freely of itself in your back garden.

To make it set up firmly like jam, you need to add apples or gooseberries, something with more pectin. A very soft rhubarb topping is delicious, however, more like a conserve than a firm jam. This recipe makes one jar of gingery, tart jam, greenish and faintly streaked with pink that is bliss on hot buttered toast.

*Makes 2 cups*

**3 cups sliced rhubarb (from about 1 pound of stalks)**

**1 cup sugar**

**½ cup candied ginger in syrup, chopped fine**

1  Put the rhubarb in a large saucepan with the sugar and bring to a boil over medium-high heat. Simmer gently until the rhubarb is softened and falling apart, and the mixture is thickened, about 15 to 20 minutes.

2  Stir the chopped ginger and its syrup into the rhubarb. Ladle into a clean, glass pint jar and let cool completely before sealing. Store in the refrigerator, where it will last about 2 weeks.

## Rhubarb and Orange Jam

Leave out the ginger and add the zest of 1 orange instead.

## Rhubarb and Raisin Jam

Leave out the ginger and add 1/2 cup raisins to the pot along with the rhubarb and sugar.

# LEMON CURD

In my childhood, a jar of lemon curd was a great treat. My dad liked it so he often brought some home, and we'd try to eat as much of it as we could spread on hot buttered toast before he clapped the lid on the jar. It's so easy to make at home I wonder why, intrepid cook that he was, he used to buy it. It's kind of like the filling for a lemon meringue pie, but while the pie filling has cornstarch as a base, lemon curd has butter as a base. You can make good lime curd by swapping in an equal amount of lime juice and zest instead of lemon, but orange curd is oddly unsuccessful—perhaps not tart enough.

Makes 1 generous cupful

3 egg yolks
Zest and juice of 3 large lemons
½ cup sugar
¼ cup (½ stick) butter, cut into
   4 pieces

1   Put the egg yolks, lemon zest and juice, and the sugar in a heatproof bowl. Set it over a pot of simmering water, being sure the water doesn't touch the bottom of the bowl. Whisk until thickened and lightened in color, about 10 minutes.

2   Remove from heat and whisk in the butter, one piece at a time.

3   Turn into a bowl or a clean jar. Cover and let cool. The curd will thicken as it cools. Store for up to two weeks in the refrigerator.

# ONION MARMALADE

Sometimes called onion compote, this typical Irish condiment is sweet and sour, almost like a chutney. (The addition of a handful of raisins would make it even more so.) However, the texture is less chunky than chutney, making onion marmalade more spreadable and definitely multi-purpose. Cold out of the jar, it's a great relish on cheese or beef sandwiches, and it's an ideal accompaniment to pâté (not to mention foie gras). You can also add a dollop to meat soups or sauces, or spread it on top of a grilled chicken breast. Warmed slightly and smeared on hot buttered toast, it's a snack that will make your toes curl with pleasure.

Makes about 2 cups

4 large yellow onions, thinly sliced
1 cup sugar
2 cups apple cider vinegar
½ cup red wine vinegar
1 tablespoon salt
1 teaspoon freshly ground black pepper
¼ teaspoon ground cloves

1   Combine all ingredients in a large, heavy-bottomed saucepan over medium heat. Bring to a boil, then reduce heat to very low and cook, stirring occasionally, for 45 to 60 minutes, until onions are tender and marmalade is thick.

2   Taste and adjust seasoning before storing in a glass jar. This will keep in the refrigerator for more than a month.

# GREEN TOMATO CHUTNEY

My dad liked to make green tomato chutney, and I surmise now it was because we rarely got enough sun in summer to ripen the tomatoes in our garden! Even so, the chutney went down well on cheese sandwiches or as a condiment alongside curries, fried fish, roast chicken, or with ham. It's sweet, tangy, pungent, and bright—everything you need to perk up your taste buds. This makes a small enough quantity to store in the fridge and use up fast so you don't have to process it in a canning bath.

*Makes about 3 cups*

1 pound green tomatoes (4 to 5 medium tomatoes), cored and diced

1 large red onion, chopped

2 cups white vinegar

1 cup golden raisins

1 cup light brown sugar

2 teaspoons salt

½ teaspoon cayenne pepper

½ teaspoon ground cloves

1  Put all the ingredients in a large, heavy saucepan over medium-high heat. Bring to a boil, then reduce heat and simmer for 50 to 60 minutes, until the tomato and onion are tender and the sauce is thickened. (If it thickens too fast, reduce the heat and add a little bit of water.)

2  Spoon into a quart jar or a couple of pint jars, seal, and refrigerate for up to a month.

## Spice Turnover

For the best flavor, be sure to use very fresh cloves. The Irish use cloves frequently, in drinks such as hot whiskey and especially in holiday baking, so the jars sitting in their cabinets have a higher turnover rate and tend to be very fresh. When you open your cloves, you should smell a fresh, pungent, spicy whiff, not a faded scent.

# BREAD SAUCE

This is another food that is consumed throughout the British Isles, not just in Ireland, but it's definitely a favorite in Ireland, served with sliced ham or boiled bacon (see p. 121). It's a creamy white sauce made of white breadcrumbs and milk that's been infused with onion, cloves, and bay leaves. The flavor is subtle but no less potent for that. Bread sauce is common enough that you can buy it in packets, but there's nothing like the homemade version. Be sure to use a good, hearty white bread without sugar, not a sweetened processed variety.

Makes about 2 cups
1 medium yellow onion
10 whole cloves
1½ cups milk
½ cup heavy cream
1 bay leaf
¾ cup fresh white bread crumbs
2 tablespoons butter
Salt and freshly ground black pepper

1   Peel and halve the onion. Stud the cut side of each half with 5 cloves. Put the onion halves in a large saucepan and cover with the milk, cream, and bay leaf. Bring to a boil over medium-high heat, then instantly turn off the heat, put a lid on the pot, and leave for 15 minutes.

2   Remove and discard the onion halves and the bay leaf. Stir in the bread crumbs, beating until thick and smooth. Season to taste with salt and pepper. Serve warm.

# ONION SAUCE

If you're not serving Parsley Sauce with bacon, this is the other go-to sauce. The onions are not browned and caramelized, just softened very slowly in butter so when flour and milk are added, they make a gentle, very aromatic white sauce. It's also excellent with Roast Leg of Lamb (p. 112) or Grilled Lamb Chops (p. 118) as a change from Mint Sauce.

*Makes about 2½ cups*
**¼ cup (½ stick) butter**
**2 large yellow onions, thinly sliced**
**2 tablespoons flour**
**1½ cups milk**
**¼ teaspoon freshly grated nutmeg**
**Salt and pepper**

1   In a large saucepan over medium-low heat, melt the butter. Stir in the onions to coat with butter, then cover the pan with a lid and cook for 12 to 15 minutes until the onions are completely tender but not at all browned. Check them once or twice. If the onions are browning, move the pan off the heat and add a tablespoon of water. Stir to cool slightly, then reduce the heat and continue cooking.

2   Sprinkle the flour over the onions, stirring to combine. Add the milk slowly, stirring constantly to prevent lumps. Bring the milk to a boil, then reduce heat and simmer very gently for 3 to 4 minutes. Season with nutmeg, salt, and plenty of black pepper.

# PARSLEY SAUCE

The chicken stock and lemon juice elevate this from just being white sauce with green stuff. It has a delicate flavor that brings out the natural sweetness in boiled bacon, sliced ham, or fish.

Makes about 3 cups
¼ cup (½ stick) butter
3 tablespoons flour
2 cups milk
1 cup chicken stock
⅓ cup finely chopped fresh parsley leaves
Juice of 1 lemon
Salt and pepper

1   In a medium saucepan over medium-low heat, melt the butter. Add the flour and cook, stirring for 1 to 2 minutes. Do not let the butter brown.

2   Slowly add the milk and chicken stock, whisking constantly to prevent lumps from forming. Increase the heat to medium and cook, stirring for 6 to 7 minutes, until the sauce is bubbling and thickened.

3   Stir in the parsley and lemon juice, and season liberally with salt and pepper.

Clockwise from top: Mint Sauce, Marie Rose Sauce, Parsley Sauce

# MINT SAUCE

The bright green, sweet mint jelly Americans sometimes eat with lamb is unknown in Ireland. Our mint sauce is sharp and savory, a mélange of fresh mint, vinegar, and just a little sugar. It's also very thin, to be spooned over or alongside beautiful slices of pink lamb.

*Makes about 1 cup*
**2 cups fresh mint, finely chopped**
**⅓ cup boiling water**
**3 tablespoons sugar**
**½ cup white wine vinegar**
**¼ teaspoon salt**

1   Place mint leaves in a small bowl and pour boiling water over them. Leave to steep for about 30 minutes.

2   Add sugar, vinegar, and salt, and mix well.

# MARIE ROSE SAUCE

Pale orange and tangy, this is the classic sauce to serve with cooked prawns, either plain boiled ones or those gorgeous deep-fried Dublin Bay Scampi (p. 101). It's mainly mayonnaise, a little ketchup, and some Tabasco. If it looks familiar to Americans, that's because you already have a very similar sauce that goes under the name of Thousand Island Dressing. An important note: in Ireland, it's not "Muh-REE Rose Sauce." It's "MARR-ee Rose Sauce."

*Makes 1 ¼ cups*
**1 cup mayonnaise**
**¼ cup ketchup**
**2 tablespoons lemon juice**
**4 to 6 drops Tabasco (or to taste)**

1   Blend together. Serve at once or refrigerate.

# ACKNOWLEDGMENTS

With thanks to my father, Kevin Bowers, who taught me so much about food and cooking with his unbridled enthusiasm in the kitchen, and to my mother, Mary Bowers, for so much help and for sharing her memories while I was creating this book. My brothers, Brian, Des, and Andrew Bowers, supported me in so many ways, with memories, techniques, and technical help. Particular thanks to Brian for accompanying me on a trip around Ireland, and thanks to John Reid for the use of his cottage in Glengarriff, County Cork (and to Eileen at the Blue Loo who provided advice and good food).

Deepest gratitude to Muireann Noonan and Tony Collins, who generously and without complaint allowed the unlimited (and, for a time, the constant) use of their kitchen in Dublin and also their kitchen in Offaly for nearly all the food prep and photography (as well as lots of props and lots of good food and drink!). Special thanks and kisses for Síofra and Déidinn Collins for all the enthusiasm, the entertaining comments, and the fabulous baking. Many thanks to Angelica Stefanuca, who has the soul of a food stylist and kept bringing just the right cloth or dish at the moment I wanted it.

My editor Jenn McCartney and the whole team at Skyhorse have been wonderful from day one, and I'm so glad to be working with you all. Warm thanks to my agent, Jennifer Griffin at MBG Literary Management, who made this whole book possible.

Finally, words aren't even necessary to convey my thanks to my wife, Sharon Bowers, indispensable in this as in all things.